T0156842

Integrative Dual Diagnosis

TREATMENT

Approach to an Individual with

ALCOHOLISM

and Coexisting Endogenous

DEPRESSION

Dr. Michael Mullan

iUniverse LLC
Bloomington

INTEGRATIVE DUAL DIAGNOSIS TREATMENT
APPROACH TO AN INDIVIDUAL WITH ALCOHOLISM
AND COEXISTING ENDOGENOUS DEPRESSION

Copyright © 1996, 2014 Dr. Michael Mullan.

All rights reserved. No part of this book may be used or reproduced by
any means, graphic, electronic, or mechanical, including photocopying,
recording, taping or by any information storage retrieval system
without the written permission of the publisher except in the case
of brief quotations embodied in critical articles and reviews.

iUniverse books may be ordered through booksellers or by contacting:

iUniverse LLC
1663 Liberty Drive
Bloomington, IN 47403
www.iuniverse.com
1-800-Authors (1-800-288-4677)

Because of the dynamic nature of the Internet, any web addresses or
links contained in this book may have changed since publication and
may no longer be valid. The views expressed in this work are solely those
of the author and do not necessarily reflect the views of the publisher,
and the publisher hereby disclaims any responsibility for them.

Any people depicted in stock imagery provided by Thinkstock are models,
and such images are being used for illustrative purposes only.
Certain stock imagery © Thinkstock.

ISBN: 978-1-4917-3668-5 (sc)
ISBN: 978-1-4917-3667-8 (hc)
ISBN: 978-1-4917-3666-1 (e)

Library of Congress Control Number: 2014910426

Printed in the United States of America.

iUniverse rev. date: 08/06/2014

INTEGRATIVE DUAL DIAGNOSIS TREATMENT APPROACH TO AN INDIVIDUAL WITH ALCOHOLISM AND COEXISTING ENDOGENOUS DEPRESSION

This case study focuses on an individual who was dually diagnosed with alcoholism and coexisting endogenous depression. The identified patient was a forty-three year old male who presented to inpatient treatment for alcoholism. The patient had an extensive history of alcohol abuse. Upon intake into treatment, the patient reported that he had three previous unsuccessful treatment episodes for his alcoholism. The patient also reported that he had been diagnosed with depression two years prior to entering this inpatient treatment program. The patient stated that despite his best efforts he was unable to maintain abstinence for more than a three-month period. The patient was separated from his wife and two children. The patient's medical license had also been suspended until he completed treatment for his alcoholism and depression, along with successful completion of a required diversion program.

The theoretical orientation used for treatment was the Integrative Dual Diagnosis Model.. This model addresses both disorders independently and concurrently, recognizing the need for chemotherapy for the treatment of depression, while integrating the twelve step model of recovery addressing the patient's alcoholism. Following an intensive sixty day program, the patient made the transition to a less-restrictive outpatient program for an additional sixty days.

The patient, at the time of this writing, had been abstinent from alcohol for one year and was continuing with his chemotherapy for his depression. The patient remained in an ongoing diversion program for the State Medical Board for reinstatement of his medical licence.

Doctor Michael Mullan is a Licensed Clinical Psychologist who recently retired from the State of California Department of Corrections. Prior to his work in corrections Dr. Mullan worked for many years in the field of addictions. He was pioneer in the field of dual diagnosis treatment of alcoholics and drug addicted individuals with co-existing mental illness. Dr Mullan was instrumental in developing one of the first dual diagnosis programs while working at Cedar House Rehabilitation Center in Bloomington California. Cedar House is a 125 bed drug and alcohol rehabilitation center serving both the indigent population as well as private pay patients. When Dr. Mullan first arrived at the facility it was strictly a 12 step based program which believed that giving patients any type of medication would be counter indicated for their recovery. Dr. Mullan states that he believed that treating the addict/alcoholic addiction alone was not the answer for a health recovery program as witnessed by the extremely high relapse rates and return to treatment. In 1995 Dr. Mullan was determined to focus on the much larger problem of treating not only the addiction to alcohol and drugs but to also treat the underlying psychological problems which many of the patients appeared to be suffering from. Dr. Mullan began to set up linkages with Riverside and San Bernardino County offices of alcohol and drug programs, as well as both counties Mental Health programs. It was Dr. Mullan's contention that if an individual was suffering with an underlying psychological problem that was not addressed in treatment that the prognosis for recovery were very poor. In the following years both San Bernardino and Riverside Counties joined in this effort by providing Mental Health practitioners to come to the facility on a weekly basis to provide adjunct therapy to their respective patients. The program turned out to be a hallmark success and a prototype for other programs to follow in the years to come. Dr. Mullan was then asked to sit on the Board of Directors at the University of California Riverside Extension Program to develop the first dual diagnosis certification program in the United States. Dr. Mullan also taught numerous class's in the program from 1996 through 1999.

In 1997 Dr. Mullan was a keynote presenter on dual diagnosis for the National Association of Drug Court Professionals "NADCP" 3rd Annual Training Conference at the Biltmore Hotel in Los Angeles. This conference had hundreds of Judges and Attorneys from all over the United States developing Drug Court programs. DR. Mullan has been a featured guest on both radio and television programs in Southern California. Dr. Mullan currently lives with his wife in Coalinga California, Dr. Mullan is on Staff with Adventist Health Community Care as well as Coalinga Regional Medical Center and maintains a private practice in Coalinga California.

DEDICATION

In loving memory of my Mother and Father, Elrene Mullan,, and Fracis John Mullan who both instilled in me the necessity of a Higher Education, the quest to seek answers and solutions. But above all to remain humble and compassionate to those in need. Thank you both for your love and support.

ACKNOWLEDGMENTS

I would like to take this opportunity to express my appreciation to a number of individuals without whose help and support this book would not have been possible. Thanks to Dr. Gary Lawson and Dr. Dennis Smith for their guidance and support. Dr. Gary Lawson has been a longtime Mentor. His knowledge, expertise, and guidance throughout the years has been inspirational.

I would like to express my loving appreciation to my wonderful wife Wanna, for her love, encouragement, and sacrifice, over the past years. Without her encouragement this road would have been a lot harder to travel, as she was there for me through the most difficult years of my life.

I would like to thank the staff and management of Cedar House Rehabilitation Center for their support. Thanks to George W. for his willingness to participate in this project; he truly is a remarkable man.

A special thanks to J.C., A.D., and B.C.; without their help and guidance this project would surely never have happened.

CONTENTS

Chapter

1. **INTRODUCTION** 1

    Project Overview 1

2. **REVIEW OF THE LITERATURE** 5

    Theories of Etiology 5

    Biological Factors 6

    Psychosocial Factors 8

    Alcoholism Theories and Views on the Etiology 12

    Alcoholics Anonymous Model 13

    Psychoanalytic Perspective 15

    Medical Model Concept.. 16

    Family Interaction Concept 17

    Behavioral Theory..17

    Sociological Concept 19

    Transactional Analysis Concept 21

    Depression and Substance Abuse 22

    Depression and Alcoholism.. 23

    Pharmacotherapy For Depressed Alcoholics 26

Comprehensive Treatment of Mood

    Disorders Within Alcoholics 28

Medications Used in the Treatment of Depression 31

Three Categories of Antidepressants 32

Tricyclics 32

MAO Inhibitors 32

Selective Serotonin Re-Uptake Inhibitors 32

3.   **MODELS OF TREATMENT FOR THE**

    DUALLY DISORDERED POPULATION 33

Moral Model 36

Learning Model 39

Disease Model 41

Self-Medication Model 44

Social Model 48

Dual Diagnosis Model 52

4.   **CASE STUDY** 57

Integrative Dual Diagnosis Treatment Approach 59

Program Description 59

Policy and Procedure For Dual Disorder Clients 60

Target Population 62

Admissions Criteria 62

Treatment Process Protocol 63

Program Evaluation and Review 67

Dual Disorders Treatment Team 67

Integrative Treatment Approach 68

Case Study: George J. - Treatment Experience..................... 70

    Phase 1. Detoxification...................................... 70

    Phase 2. Long Term Treatment,

        Assessment and Planning........................... 70

    Master Problem List 71

    Treatment Plan 1 71

    Problem No. 1... 71

    Problem No. 2:...74

    Medication Dosage and Administration..................... 75

    Problem No. 3... 76

    The Theory of Homeostasis................................... 76

    Family Constellation... 77

    Problem No. 4... 78

    Problem No. 5... 79

    Summary of Treatment Experience............................ 79

5.   **DISCUSSION** 81

References.. 85

CHAPTER 1

INTRODUCTION

Project Overview

The following case study project involves the treatment of an individual, known here as George J. (This is not the individual's true name). George was initially presented to treatment for chronic alcoholism. The patient was brought into the treatment facility by his parents. His parents stated that despite numerous treatment attempts, George had been unable to maintain any significant length of abstinence from alcohol. Prior to entering treatment, George had been treated at a local hospital for injuries sustained when he drove his bicycle over an embankment while intoxicated. His parents stated that George had been in the ditch overnight, and that he was found the following morning by a passing pedestrian. George was treated at a local hospital for his immediate medical conditions. After George's stabilization, the hospital recommended that he be referred to a treatment center for his alcoholism. During the initial intake screening process, George stated that he was a forty-two year old medical doctor, who had been unable to practice medicine for the past three years due in part to his alcoholism. George stated that he had had four previous treatment episodes for his alcoholism. He had been hospitalized two times in 1993, once in 1994, and once in 1995. The patient stated that he had also been hospitalized in a psychiatric hospital in 1993 for a period of ten days, following a failed suicide attempt. At that time George had been given two DSM IV Axis I Diagnostic codes -- Axis-I 296.3x -Major Depression Recurrent, and 303.90 - Alcoholism. Upon admission into detox, George was receiving 25 mg. doses of Librium four times per day as a preventative step down for severe alcohol withdrawal. George was also taking one 100 mg. dose of Doxopin per day, for depression. George stated that he had only taken his Doxepin on an intermittent basis since he was first prescribed the medication in 1993.

An effective treatment approach was required in order to deal with George's specific needs. Because George had two separate Axis I Diagnosis', the theoretical approach selected for this case was the Integrative Dual Diagnosis Treatment Approach.

Chapter 2 of this project will examine a review of the literature related to the clinical problems of dealing with alcoholism, and alcoholism with co-existing mental illness. Chapter 2 will review the literature for various theoretical frameworks of alcoholism, its etiology, and treatment approaches. The theoretical approaches that will be reviewed in Chapter 2 are:

1.) Alcoholics Anonymous
2.) Psychoanalytic
3.) The Medical Model
4.) Family Interaction Concept
5.) The Behavioral Model

6.) Sociological Concept

7.) Transactional Analysis

8.) Models of Treatment for the Dually Disordered Population

9.) An Integrative Dual Diagnosis Approach

Chapter 2 will also include an overview of the dually diagnosed population, i.e. individuals with substance abuse coupled with mental health problems. Because the focus of this project concerns itself with the case study of an individual with alcoholism and depression, Chapter 2 will also include an overview of the current literature on depression, and depression as it relates to alcoholism.

REVIEW OF THE LITERATURE

Theories of Etiology

In trying to identify the causes of problem drinking, some researchers have stressed the role of genetic and biochemical factors; others have pointed to psychosocial factors, viewing problem drinking as a maladaptive pattern of adjustment to the stress of life; still others have emphasized sociocultural factors, such as the availability of alcohol and the social approval of excessive drinking. As with most other forms of maladaptive behavior, it appears that there may be several types of alcoholic dependence, each with somewhat different patterns of biological, psychosocial, and sociocultural causal factors. Recently, a committee of experts from the National Academy of Sciences (Institute of Medicine, 1990) concluded that identifying a single cause for all types of alcohol problems is unlikely.

Biological Factors

In an alcohol dependent person, cell metabolism has adapted itself to the presence of alcohol in the bloodstream and now demands it for stability. When the alcohol in the bloodstream falls below a certain level, withdrawal symptoms occur. These symptoms may be relatively mild -- including a craving for alcohol, tremors, perspiration, and weakness -- or more severe; with nausea, vomiting, fever, rapid heart beat, convulsions, and hallucinations. The shortcut to ending them is to take another drink. Once this point is reached, each drink serves to reinforce alcohol seeking behavior because it reduces the unpleasant symptoms. An unusual craving could result from a genetic vulnerability. The possibility of a genetic predisposition to developing alcohol abuse problems has been widely researched. Cotton, (1979) in a review of 39 studies of families of 6251 alcoholics and 4083 non-alcoholics who had been followed over 40 years, reported that almost one third of alcoholics had at least one parent with an alcohol problem. More recently, a study of children of alcoholics by Cloninger et al. (1986) reported strong evidence for the inheritance of alcoholism. They found that for males, having one alcoholic parent increased the rate of alcoholism from 11.4 percent to 29.5 percent, and having two alcoholic parents increased the rate to 41.2 percent. For females with no alcoholic parents, the rate was 5.0 percent; for those with one alcoholic parent the rate was 9.5 percent, and for those with two alcoholic parents it was 25.0 percent. However, it should be kept in mind that the majority of individuals in the study did not have alcoholic parents. Also, such studies do not rule out environmental influences such as modeling.

Dr. Michael Mullan

One approach to understanding the precursors to alcoholism is to study the behavior of individuals who are at high risk for substance abuse but who are not yet affected by alcohol -- prealcoholic personalities. An alcohol-risk personality has been described by Finn (1990), as an individual (usually the child of an alcoholic) who has an inherited predisposition toward alcohol abuse and who is impulsive, prefers taking high risks, is emotionally unstable, has difficulty planning and organizing behavior, has problems in predicting the consequences of his or her actions, has many psychological problems, finds that alcohol is helpful in coping with stress, does not experience hangovers, and finds alcohol rewarding.

Finn et al. (1990) found that pre-alcoholic men show different physiological patterns than non-alcoholic men in several respects. Pre-alcoholic men are more sensitive to stress-response dampening (lessened experience to stress) with alcohol ingestion than non-alcoholic men. They also show different alpha wave patterns on EEG (Stewart, Finn, and Pihl, 1990). Pre-alcoholic men as defined by the personality characteristic, were found to show larger conditioned physiological responses to alcohol cues than were individuals who were considered low risk for alcoholism, according to Earlywine and Finn (1990). These results suggest that pre-alcoholic men may be more prone to develop tolerance for alcohol than low risk men. In support of possible genetic factors in alcoholism, some research has suggested that certain ethnic groups, particularly Asians and American Indians, have abnormal physiological reactions to alcohol. Fenna et al. (1971) and Wolff (1972) found that Asian and Inuit (A member of an Eskimo people) subjects showed a hypersensitive reaction, including flushing of the skin, a drop in blood pressure, and nausea, following the ingestion of alcohol. The relatively lower rates of alcoholism among Asian groups are tentatively considered to be related to a faster metabolism. However, Schaefer (1977, 1978) questioned these and other metabolism studies as a basis for interpreting cultural differences in alcoholism rates using more explicit criteria of metabolism between a group of Reddis Indians and a group of Northern European subjects. He concluded that further research into metabolism rate differences and sensitivity to alcohol needs to be integrated with studies focusing on relative stress in various cultures.

There has been evidence linking drug dependency or alcoholism with genetic factors, psychological factors, and sociocultural factors, but none of the research has demonstrated that any one of these factors is the major contributor to the etiology of chemical dependency (Lawson, Lawson and Rivers, 1996).

Psychosocial Factors

Not only do alcoholics become physiologically dependent on alcohol, but they develop powerful psychological dependence as well. Because excessive drinking is so destructive to an individual's total life adjustment, the question arises as to why psychological dependence is learned. A number of psychosocial factors have been advanced as possible answers.

Psychological Vulnerability -- Is there an "Alcoholic Personality?" -- A type of character organization that predisposes a given individual to turn to the use of alcohol rather than some other defensive pattern of coping with stress? In efforts to answer this question, investigators

Dr. Michael Mullan

have reported that potential alcoholics tend to be emotionally immature, to expect a great deal of the world, to require an inordinate amount of praise and appreciation, to react to failure with marked feelings of hurt and inferiority, to have low frustration tolerance, and to feel inadequate and unsure of their abilities to fulfill expected male or female roles. Morey, Skinner, Blashfield (1984) have shown that individuals at high risk for alcoholism development were significantly different in personality in terms of showing more impulsion and aggression, from those at low risk for abusing alcohol.

The two psychopathological conditions that have been most frequently linked to addictive disorders are depression (Lutz and Snow, 1985; Weissman et al., 1977; Woodruff et al., 1973) and antisocial personality (Cadonet et al., 1985; Seixas and Cadonet, 1974; Stabenau, 1984). By far, most of the research has related antisocial personality and addictive disorders, with about 75 to 80 percent of the studies showing an association between the two (Alterman, 1988; Grand et al., 1985). While such findings provide promising leads, it is difficult to assess the role of specific personality characteristics in the development of alcoholism. Certainly many people with similar personality characteristics do not become alcoholics, and others with dissimilar ones do. The only characteristic that appears common to the backgrounds of most problem drinking is personal maladjustment, yet most maladjusted people do not become alcoholics. An alcoholic's personality may be as much a result, as a cause of his or her dependence on alcohol. For example, the excessive use of alcohol may lead to depression, or a depressed person may turn to the excessive use of alcohol, or both.

In somewhat of a different approach to transmission of alcoholism, Lawson, et al. (1983) proposed or identified four parental types which are associated with the development of alcoholism in the offspring. They stated that alcoholics have typically had one or both parents in one or more of the following categories:

1.) The Alcoholic Parent - The child learns alcoholic behavior as a way of dealing with problems, modeling the parents' behavior.

2.) Teetotaler Parents - This parent is too rigid and has unreasonable expectations for the child, from which he eventually rebels by drinking.

3.) The Over-Demanding Parent - The stress of an overly demanding parent may result in such a low self esteem that the child turns to alcohol to feel better about himself.

4.) The Over-Protective Parent - The children of these parents never develop the self confidence necessary to deal with life's problems and may resort to alcohol as a coping mechanism.

Sociocultural theory of alcoholism is based on an ethnic group's approval/disapproval of drinking alcohol. Pittman (1967) placed cultural attitudes toward drinking on a continuum as follows: (1) abstinent culture; (2) ambivalent culture; (3) permissive culture; and (4) over-permissive culture. These attitudes reflect customs, values and sanctions of different ethnic and social groups. Thus, frequent and heavy drinking is accepted and even almost expected in some cultures. Examples include American Indians, and the Irish (McGoldrick, et al., 1982). Thus these groups tend to have more problems with alcoholism.

Dr. Michael Mullan

In contrast the authors point to the Jewish people as an example of an ethnic group which frowns upon excessive use of alcohol. The Jewish tend to emphasize intellectual achievement and pursuits, and disapprove of anything that interferes with these pursuits. Even though the Jewish do use alcohol in some of their religious ceremonies or rituals, they do not characteristically have problems with alcohol abuse as a group. Lawson, et al. (1983) identified three factors that contribute to alcohol consumption problems within a given culture. These include: (1) the degree to which the culture produces inner tension in its members; (2) the culture's attitude toward drinking; and (3) the degree to which the culture provides substitutes for alcohol usage.

The learning theory model holds that all behavior is learned through modeling and/or social reinforcement. Children who see their parents using alcohol as a coping mechanism would theoretically be more likely to model this alcohol usage for the same purpose for themselves. Also, if alcohol is effectively used to reduce situational anxiety, this is reinforcing to that individual. Thus, what works once is repeated again and again, forming a pattern that may lead to abuse and alcoholism.

Rapid social change and social disintegration also seem to foster excessive drinking. For example, the U.S. Public Health Service's Alaska Native Medical Center reported excessive drinking to be a major problem among the Inuit in many places in rural Alaska (Time and Apulzz, 1974). This problem was attributed primarily to rapid change in traditional values and ways of life, in some cases approaching social disintegration. The effect of cultural attitudes toward drinking is well illustrated by Muslims and Mormans, whose religious values prohibit the use of alcohol, and by orthodox Jews, who have traditionally limited it's use largely to religious rituals. The incidence of alcoholism among these groups is minimal. In comparison, the incidence of alcoholism is high among Europeans who comprise less than 15 percent of the world's population yet consume about half the alcohol (Sulkunen, 1976). Interestingly, Europe and six countries that have been influenced by European Culture -- Argentina, Canada, Chile, Japan, the United States, and New Zealand -- make up less than 20 percent of the world's population, yet consume 80 percent of the alcohol (Barry, 1982). The French appear to have the highest rate of alcoholism in the world, approximately 15 percent of the population. France has both the highest per capita alcohol consumption and the highest death rate from Cirrhosis of the Liver (Noble, 1979). Thus it appears that religious sanctions and social customs can determine whether alcohol is one of the coping methods commonly used in a given group or society. There appears to be many reasons why people drink, as well as many conditions that predispose individuals to do so and reinforce drinking behavior, however, the combination of factors that result in a person's becoming an alcoholic are yet unknown.

Alcoholism Theories and Views on the Etiology

In the field of alcoholism theory and treatment, a number of conceptual frameworks have been advanced, all of which purport to explain the nature of alcoholism.

One approach might define alcoholism as a disease, while another might argue that alcoholism is a bad habit or a lack of willpower. Since no one has been able to provide adequate evidence as to which conception is most valid, the way one approaches addiction is often a matter of individual preference. At various times in history, one conception will be more popular than another. Over time, some views will fall into relative disrepute often giving way to a new (and hopefully more scientifically defensible) theoretical approach. Currently, there exists in the field of addiction theory and treatment a number of theoretical approaches to addiction. Some of the most widely used approaches are (1) Alcoholics Anonymous; (2) Psychoanalytic; (3) the medical model; (4) Family interaction concept; (5) the behavioral model; and (6) the sociological concept of transactional analysis. Some are totally opposite in their respective definitions of alcoholism and theory regarding etiology, and their prescription for treatment. Others, however, are fairly similar, having only shades of differences. For the purpose of this project, some of the most widely used theoretical models will be examined in regards to theory and etiology.

Alcoholics Anonymous Model

Alcoholics Anonymous (A.A.) is the most widespread and utilized treatment approach in the field of alcoholism. A.A. was founded in 1935 by two alcoholics, anonymously named Bill Wilson and Dr. Bob Silkworth. Their idea was to develop a fellowship composed of problem drinkers who would lend each other assistance in conquering their obsession with alcohol. From the beginning, A.A.

has spawned a truly remarkable following that spans geographic, cultural, and socioeconomic lines. Nearly every community in the United States, large or small, has A.A. meetings on a regular basis. This scope is especially remarkable because A.A. is composed totally of anonymous volunteers, receives no outside funding, and has no central administration or organized leadership. Over the years, A.A. has evolved both a set of by-laws, called "Traditions," and a relatively uniform procedure of rehabilitation, known as the "Twelve Steps." In general, A.A. philosophy holds the following beliefs: (1) Alcoholism is an incurable, progressive disease that will result in death without therapeutic intervention; (2) the only remedy for alcoholism is complete abstinence from drinking; (3) once an alcoholic, always an alcoholic -- no cure is possible, only remission; and (4) no one can cure his/her own alcoholism without help (Lawson et al. 1983).

A.A. differs from many of the other theoretical approaches in its spiritual orientation, the concept of a Higher Power, and complete spiritual surrender to a Power greater than ones-self.

Etiology

It is not overly simplistic to say that the cause of alcoholism, according to the A.A. model is drinking alcohol. The reason that some people can drink and not become alcoholic while others do, is because the alcoholic is different both emotionally and/or spiritually, as well as physically. The potential alcoholic is both psychologically and biologically susceptible to becoming an alcoholic due to genetic predisposition. Drinking brings out the susceptibility in the alcoholic, but not in the normal social drinker. Though the precise, physiological factors responsible for the

Dr. Michael Mullan

alcoholic's susceptibility are not scientifically known, the proponents of the A.A. model point to the fact that different people can drink similar amounts of alcohol over the same length of time, and only some develop alcoholism. This is at least indirect evidence that the alcoholic is constitutionally different and that this difference may be an inherited physiological susceptibility. The A.A. theory indicates that once a person has become alcoholic that he will always be an alcoholic, and that the condition cannot be cured, only arrested. Therefore, A.A. believes in total abstinence from any mood altering chemical.

Psychoanalytic Perspective

The classical psychoanalytic model places heavy emphasis on unconscious motivation in human behavior. Those who adhere to this model would argue that alcoholism is the consequence of an unresolved psychological conflict which has been repressed into the unconscious. Often this unconscious conflict has its roots in early childhood. If for example, one experiences a traumatic event during the oral stage of psychosexual development, a fixation in that stage may occur. This fixation continues through adulthood if it is not resolved. Excessive drinking is often taken as an indication of one's fixation in the oral stage of psychosexual development. Another interesting theory concerning the etiology of alcoholism stemming from this model, is the idea that alcoholism is chronic suicide. The reasoning is that since there is such a high incidence of suicide among alcoholics, the alcoholic is a suicidal person. But since he does not want to face up to taking his life, he does it slowly by drinking himself to death. The reason for wanting to commit suicide is some unconscious conflict which is probably rooted in the distant past. Freud (1930) postulated that if this conflict is not resolved, both alcoholism and suicidal tendencies will persist.

Medical Model Concept

Alcoholism is a progressive disease having physiological determinants. Alcoholics are people whose body chemistry makes them susceptible to becoming addicted to alcohol. This physiological susceptibility may be inherited.

Etiology

There are at least two explanations of etiology from the medical model. The first is that certain people are born with a body chemistry that makes them potential alcoholics. When these people begin to drink, the interaction of alcohol with the susceptible physiological make-up results in the symptoms of alcoholism. The second explanation is that long years of drinking may alter the biochemistry of some people which in turn causes further excessive and uncontrollable drinking characteristics of alcoholism. Though there are differences between these explanations in terms of the initial cause of alcoholism (whether susceptible body chemistry precedes alcoholic drinking or whether excessive drinking precedes altered body chemistry), the final result is the same -- alcoholic drinking having a physiological basis.

Family Interaction Concept

Of the models discussed thus far, only the A.A. model emphasized the importance of social relationships in the treatment of alcoholism. The family interaction model places sole importance on the alcoholic's relationships with others (particularly family relations), in answering questions about etiology, treatment and prognosis.

Etiology

Since the relationship between the alcoholic and other family members is seen as circular and mutually reinforcing, it is difficult to pinpoint the original cause of alcoholism. However, once the alcoholic process has begun, one is able to identify the specific roles each family member plays in sustaining and perpetuating the illness. Roles such as the disgraced parents, the self-pitying spouse, and the neglected children are often apparent to the trained observer. Attempts to change the roles therapeutically often meet with a good deal of resistance, signifying the functions the respective roles serve both for the individual members and the family as a whole.

Behavioral Theory

The behaviorist is reluctant to use the term alcoholic because it has disease connotations. Rather, the behaviorist would prefer to speak of drinking behavior that results in problems with living or more simply, problem drinking. The reason is that the behaviorist does not conceive of alcoholism (if we are permitted to use the term) as being caused by physiological factors such as inherited biochemical susceptibility, but would contend that factors outside the person (environmental factors) like rewards for heavy drinking, cause problem drinking. This general denial that alcoholism is a disease has created a good deal of controversy in the field of alcoholism and its treatment.

Etiology

Behaviorists (operant behaviorists) are less interested in the original cause of a person's heavy drinking than those factors that sustain it. Heavy or problem drinking is sustained because it is reinforced. A reinforcer is anything that increases the probability of the problem drinking occurring in the future. Events like social approval from peers are important reinforcers that perpetuate problem drinking. Heavy alcohol use can also be maintained by negative reinforcers. When heavy drinking continues because it removes unwanted experiences like anxiety, the heavy drinking is being negatively reinforced. The use of the term "negative" refers to the fact that heavy drinking does away with (negates) anxiety. Nevertheless, the problem drinking is being reinforced since its probability of future occurrence is increased. In general, problem drinking is instigated and maintained by a combination of positive and negative reinforcers.

Dr. Michael Mullan

Sociological Concept

The models reviewed thus far have focused, for the most part, on individual behavior. They have provided differing ideas about the etiology and treatment of alcoholism that can be applied to particular people. Questions like "Why is John an alcoholic but not his friend?" are questions they are designed to answer. The sociological model shifts the level of inquiry to larger segments of society. Rather than explaining differences in individual drinking behavior, the sociological model is more appropriate for explaining gross differences in alcoholism between social classes or between ethnic groups or religions. Though not exclusively, the sociologist is interested in differences in rates of alcoholism between and within various social categories in society (Fingarette, 1988).

Etiology

The strain theorist would see alcoholism as a result of an imbalance in the social structure. Menton (1983) has provided one of the most popular expositions of this thesis. He theorizes that at least in American society, there are a set of common goals toward which everyone in society aspires. Material health such as a nice home, a good car and expensive clothes are examples of common goals toward which Americans aspire. Even though everyone wants these things, not everyone has an equal opportunity to achieve them. Due to artificial barriers like race discrimination in education and employment, certain segments of society (mostly racial and ethnic minorities) are systematically excluded from legitimate opportunities to achieve societal goals. Such opportunity blockage creates a condition of social structural strain. This imbalance between wanted goals and lack of opportunity creates a sense of hopelessness and helplessness. Alcoholic drinking may provide a means of escape from this unsatisfactory life condition. According to the theory, the lower classes experience a greater degree of blocked opportunity and hence should account for a disproportionate amount of the alcoholic drinking.

As mentioned, the labeling theorist is less interested in the original cause of a person's problem drinking than with what others decide to do about it. However, once the label of alcoholic is attached to someone, the labeling theorist becomes interested in the consequences of that label. Stated another way, the labeling theorist would argue that the "disease label may have disease consequences" (Roman and Trice, 1968). This is not to deny a possible pharmacological basis for alcoholism. But to assign the sick role to someone who is not physically addicted may very well create a self-fulfilling prophecy. This occurs because the sick role assignment (labeling a person alcoholic) absolves the person of responsibility of his drinking behavior. If a person no longer feels responsible (in control) for his drinking, the tendency is to become the very thing he is labeled. The labeling theorist would argue that to label a person alcoholic (even if you are trying to help) may very well create the thing you are trying to prevent. This position stands of course, directly opposite to the Alcoholics Anonymous model and has created a great deal of controversy in the field.

Transactional Analysis Concept

The transactional approach to understanding human behavior was popularized by Eric Benne in his book entitled, "Games People Play." Later, Claude Steiner became the leader in applying basic concepts of transactional analysis to the understanding and treatment of alcoholism. His article entitled "The Alcoholic Game" (Steiner, 1969) is considered requisite reading for all subscribers to the T.A. approach to alcoholism theory and therapy.

Definition

The transactional analyst defines alcoholism as a game rather than a disease. In fact, it is argued that physiological addiction is somewhat inconsequential in the maintenance of alcoholic drinking. Rather, heavy alcohol use is sustained merely because it results in social reinforcers (Strokes) conferred on the alcoholic by those engaged in the alcoholics network of interpersonal relationships Benjamin (1982), Carson (1969, 1979), Kiesler (1983), Leary (1957), and Wiggins (1982).

Etiology

As implied by the definition of alcoholism, the source of alcoholic behavior is not to be found in biochemical factors, but in interpersonal transactions. To this degree, the theory of etiology bears similarities to the behavioral approach. The T.A. therapist holds that alcoholics begin with fundamental life scripts which are dominant conceptions of self. They attempt to validate these identities by getting others to participate in interpersonal transactions (games) that serve to reaffirm the initial self-conceptions. As it applies to alcoholism, an individual's script might be "I'm not a worthy person," and its corollary "Neither is anyone else." The interpersonal game might involve the alcoholic's attempt to expose and discredit others who may think they are okay. He will attempt to entice them into one of the alcoholic roles. Roles such as the powerless rescuer, the patsy, or just another alcoholic serve to "stroke" the alcoholic and keep the game going.

Depression and Substance Abuse

The relationship between affective disorder and alcoholism has been studied extensively (Chapman and Chapman, 1987). The positive relationship between affective disorder and alcoholism can be inferred from the finding of a high incidence of affective disorder in the families of alcoholics (Winokur, Clayton, and Reich, cited in Mayfield, 1985; Winokur, Reich, Rimmer, and Pitts, cited in Mayfield, 1985). There is also a high rate of suicidal attempts and compilation with both affective disorder and alcoholism. As Mueser et al. (1990, p. 110) noted: "Studies reporting on the prevalence of affective disorder in alcoholic populations give ratio rates of 5-9% while conversely 8-36% of manic-depressives are said to exhibit coexisting alcoholism." Other researchers (e.g., Zimberg, 1985) have provided somewhat varying figures. Addiction to substances other than alcohol and the relationship of these addictions to depression have been less well researched.

Depression and Alcoholism

There has been an association established between depression and alcoholism for a relatively long period of time, particularly in terms of suicide (Mueser et al., 1990). It should be noted that there are relatively consistent test data that suggest that alcohol abuse leads to elevated scores on the depression scale of the Minnesota Multiphasic Personality Inventory (MMPI). However, in the majority of cases, the score on the depression scale declines as the individual begins to recover from the toxic state of alcohol abuse. This indicates that there is probably some depression brought on by alcohol abuse itself. This depression clears up as individuals begin to cope with the toxic state of alcohol abuse and resolve their guilt over the harm they may have done to significant people in their lives. These individuals typically show no history of depression. The type of depression that usually occurs in reaction to the physical and psychological consequences of drinking is reactive, or exogenous depression.

Endogenous depression can be defined as depression that is not related to a precipitating event, does not seem to be improved by a change in the person's situation, and reoccurs over the person's life cycle. There is sometimes, but not always, a family history of depression that can be readily documented. There are two types of endogenous depression identified in the Journal of Abnormal Psychology (1996). The first type, unipolar depression, refers to a disorder that is expressed by deep depression and melancholia. Persons may, over their life span, move from a mood that would be classified as "normal" to severe depression several times.

The second type of endogenous depression is called "Bipolar Disorder" and has been referred to in earlier classification schemes in the Diagnostic and Statistical Manual as manic-depressive disorder.

Individuals show a typical cycle of moving from normal affect to manic-like behavior where they sleep very little, are very active, talk and move constantly, and show a rapid shift in ideas and verbal material. They are so active that they may exhaust the onlooker. They also may have grandiose schemes and be temporarily amusing to the people with whom they interact, although eventually they push the limits too far and are perceived as rude and insensitive. This part of the cycle is then followed by depression. The depression cycle shows the same or similar type of depression as the unipolar depression. Sometimes it may show a typical pattern of going from normal behavior to manic and then depression. Finally then, the person will return again to normal mood state.

Mayfield (1985) noted that the co-occurrence of alcoholism and affective disorder is a more recent finding. For example, Mayfield and Coleman (1968) found alcoholism in 20% of their bipolar patients. For individuals whose primary diagnosis is alcoholism, Mayfield (1985) reported less striking by reliable coincidences of about 7% to 9% who were also diagnosed as having an affective disorder.

Perhaps one of the major hypotheses regarding affective disorders in general and alcoholism is that they may reflect the same underlying problem in different ways, i.e. expressed as alcoholism in men and depression in women. This hypothesis has been generated from the research on family coincidences of alcoholism and depression noted above. As Mayfield (1985) indicated, Winokur and his colleagues used the research on concurrence of depression and alcoholism "to devise a hypothetical subdivision of unipolar affective disorder" Mayfield (1985, p. 71). These included:

1.) Depressive spectrum disease, a serious unipolar depression occurring in a person with a first degree relative suffering from either alcoholism or antisocial personality with or without a first degree relation with unipolar depression.

2.) Familial pure depressive disease, occurring in an individual with a first degree relative suffering only from unipolar depression.

3.) Sporadic depressive disease, occurring in the absence of any psychiatric illness among first degree relatives.

It is the first, depressive spectrum disease that suggests a common underlying familial attribute that may be expressed as either unipolar affective disease or alcoholism.

One issue that must be addressed is the fact that alcohol is used by many people to alter their mood state. The self-reports of drinkers when experimentally intoxicated in a laboratory setting show improved mood at low levels of alcohol intoxication. However, this change in mood does not appear to be euphoric and seems to be below the positive affect changes reported for cocaine or amphetamines. At high levels of intoxication, there is a deterioration in mood.

These findings do not support the notion that the alcoholic drinker abuses alcohol to reach a euphoric state. Indeed, research on alcoholics suggest that alcoholics in laboratory settings have deterioration in mood (i.e. become more depressed and anxious) under chronic heavy alcohol intake (Mayfield, 1987). These results have been replicated by several other researchers. Mood changes have been observed to proceed to the point of a severe depressive syndrome with suicidal ideation. A question arises. Why do alcoholics who suffer this depressive affect continue to drink? One possibility is that although they are not finding euphoria from their drinking, they may be relieved from dysphoria (a sense of melancholia, sadness or depression) (i.e. returning to a more moderate and mid-range mood state). That this may occur has been supported to some degree by laboratory research on acute severe depression (Mayfield and Allen, 1967). The subjects in these studies showed profound improvement in most mood factors after mild acute intoxication. While these findings suggest that alcohol can have positive effects on severely depressed people, it was also found that those subjects who had a history of excessive drinking showed much less improvement than did subjects who had never been excessive drinkers.

Pharmacotherapy For Depressed Alcoholics

Having a dual diagnosis usually means a longer period of treatment than would be true for a person with just one of the problems (Valiant, 1983). This is especially true when compared with the treatment time of the typical alcohol program. Within general alcohol treatment programs, there is also a concern with the use of psychotropic drugs as a part of treatment (i.e. that they should not be used at all if their use can be avoided). Despite these concerns, there have been several ways that pharmacotherapy has been used with depressed alcoholics. It is important to note that the alcoholic should be sober and abstinent before any psychotropic drugs are prescribed. In terms of the neurotic, or reactive (exogenous) depression so often seen in alcoholics overall (Whiffen, 1991, 1993; Whiffen and Gotlib, 1993) found that Phenothiazine and Tricyclic antidepressants in low dosages may be of assistance. These two types of medication were more effective than Diazepam in producing relief from symptoms in separate groups of detoxified alcoholics with Anxiety Depression Syndrome. This is an important finding since many people feel that the prescribing of minor tranquilizers is not a realistic treatment option in view of the addiction potential of these drugs. In general, it can be said that research has not supported the initial enthusiasm for treating depressed alcoholics with antidepressants (O'Sullivan, 1984).

A similar finding seems to have been established for the use of Lithium Carbonate in the treatment of depression in alcoholics. While this treatment does seem to be effective with patients who have a primary affective disorder, it is not useful with reactive depression. Severe depressive disorders occur only occasionally in alcoholics. When these disorders do occur, the pattern of using Lithium treatment is similar to that followed in treating nonalcoholics with an affective disorder (O'Sullivan, 1984). When treating the alcoholic with depression, it is frequently helpful to have as specific a description of the client as possible. Mayfield (1985) outlined four subtypes of depression in alcoholics that need to be considered:

1.) Depression developed in reaction to chronic intoxication (disappears promptly upon cessation of drinking.)
2.) Suicidal/reactive depression.

3.) Depression that might be called characterological depression, which is long standing and independent of life events ("Normally" a depressed individual).
4.) Severe affective disorder or endogenous depression.

The first of these is not helped by medication. It is only the last type, (i.e. severe affective disorder) for which medication may be helpful (Mayfield, 1985).

Comprehensive Treatment of Mood Disorders Within Alcoholics

The preferred ordering of treatment with the dual diagnosis of alcoholism and depression was commented on by O'Sullivan (1984). He suggested that control over problem drinking takes priority in the early phase of treatment. Only after the alcoholic is abstinent can a true picture of the underlying pathology emerge and be dealt with over time. Once abstinence has been accomplished, the type of treatment offered will depend on many factors, including the patient's capacity for insight, the intactness of the personality, and the presence or absence of intellectual impairment. O'Sullivan suggested obtaining a collateral history from a significant other to help deal with the issue of denial or memory lapses by the patient. The use of the family members and other possible sources of support were also encouraged. Support from others is particularly helpful in dealing with the reactive depression found in alcoholics suffering with guilt related to drinking-associated actions. This is especially an issue when the alcoholic is forced to deal with these guilt feelings without the support of alcohol.

Blume (1985) discussed dealing with depression in the group psychotherapy session. She suggested that the therapist make an effort to draw persons out slowly so that they may express their feelings, including crying or mourning, if appropriate. She noted that depressed persons are usually very quiet in the group. Once the depression and its possible causes are expressed, the group can sympathize with depressed persons and comfort them. The group can then help such patients win a series of small victories to help them gain a sense of mastery over their life and their environment. A helpful question, once the depression begins to lift is: "Do you deserve to be happy?" Once the patients admit they have that right, the leader can ask each of them to go to each member, make eye contact, and repeat: "I deserve to be happy." According to Blume, "Not guilty" is an excellent motto for some depressed people in such group sessions.

While reactive depression is a frequent occurrence in both sexes, the presence of a major affective disorder is much more common in female alcoholics. For example, Zimbers (1985) indicated that only 5% or fewer of male alcoholics have major affective disorders, while 25% to 50% of female alcoholics may suffer from this type of problem. He suggested treatment with Lithium Carbonate for these patients. A similar finding regarding the rates of severe affective disorders in women was made by Tamerin (1985).

One result of depression in female alcoholics is a syndrome called "Inhibited sexual desire." Littrel (1991) outlined ways of treating this disorder. His techniques are included here because some of them are quite effective in dealing with depression in general in both men and women. Powell suggested that the therapist intervene to disrupt depression in a number of ways:

1.) Behavioral interventions: These include increasing positive reinforcers, dealing with learned helplessness, reducing stress, and teaching problem-solving skills.

2.) Affective interventions: These include dealing with anger, resentment, and guilt; reducing passivity and distrust; and dealing with negative self-fulfilling prophecies.

3.) Cognitive interventions: These include eliminating negative thoughts, teaching thought-stopping techniques, reforming myths and conditions, and dealing with boredom.

4.) Systematic relational interventions: These include modifying relationships and roles/expectations, changing destructive interactions, and reducing tendencies toward being a workaholic.

SOME OF THE MOST WIDELY PRESCRIBED MEDICATIONS
USED IN THE TREATMENT OF DEPRESSION

Tricyclics

Trade	Generic
Asendin	Amoxapine
Elavil	Amitriptyline
Ludiomil	Maprotiline
Norpramine	Desipramine
Pamelor	Nortriptyline
Sinequan	Doxepin
Surmontil	Trimipramine
Tofranil	Imipramine

MAO Inhibitors

Furoxone	Furazolidone
Marplan	Isocarboxazide
Nardil	Phenelzine
Parnate	Tranylcypromine
Pargyline	Eutonyl

Selective Serotonin Re-Uptake Inhibitors (SSRI's)

Fluoxetine	Prozac
Fluvoxamine	Luvox
Paroxetine	Paxil
Sertraline	Zoloft

Three Categories of Antidepressants

1.) **Tricyclics:** Antidepressants which work by potentiating the activity of Norepinephrine by blocking its re-uptake at the presynaptic membrane; also appear to interfere with the re-uptake of serotonin. Most effective in treating unipolar and endogenous depression. Examples are Trofanil, Norpramine and Elavil.

2.) **MAO Inhibitors:** Antidepressant drugs which antagonize MAO (Monoamine Oxidase), an enzyme that metabolically degrades catecholamine and indoleamine transmitter substances within presynaptic nerve terminals. Appear most effective in treating "Atypical Depression." Highly toxic; can be fatal if an overdose is taken. Must be mixed with foods containing Tyramine and certain other drugs.

3.) **Selective Serotonin Re-uptake Inhibitors (SSRI's):** The second-generation antidepressants SSRI's are drugs that exert more specific effects on a single Neurotransmitter. For example, Fluoxetine (Prozac) blocks the re-uptake of Serotonin by the Presynaptic terminal. The side effects of such drugs are more limited and more predictable than those of standard tricyclics and MAOI's, which may affect four or more Neurotransmitters (Feigner et al., 1991).

CHAPTER 3

MODELS OF TREATMENT FOR THE DUALLY DISORDERED POPULATION

Models of chemical dependency treatment can be divided for the purpose of classification, in basic and integrative models (Table 2). The five basic models are the moral model, the learning model, the disease model, the self-medication model, and the social model. Each of these basic models will be described in terms of the assumptions they make about the etiology of chemical dependency and the goals and strategies they suggest for treatment.

TABLE 1

Classification of Chemical Dependency Treatment Models

Basic Models (Single Focus)	Integrative Models (Multifocus)
Moral	Alcoholics Anonymous
Learning	Dual Diagnosis
Disease	Biopsychosocial
Self Medication	Multivariant
Social	

Permission to reprint granted by source: Journal of Substance Abuse Treatment, Vol.6, pp 147-157, 1989

The advantages and disadvantages of each model for treatment will also be examined.

Integrative models combine or integrate elements from the basic models. Alcoholics Anonymous, the dual diagnosis model, and the biopsychosocial model are all examples of integrative models. In contrast to the basic models, which concentrate primarily on a single treatment focus, integrative models are multifocused. For example, whereas the disease model focuses primarily on substance abuse and the self-medication model focuses primarily on underlying psychopathology, the dual diagnosis model focuses on both substance abuse and coexisting psychopathology.

The major contention of this research is that clinical work is enhanced by being flexible enough to integrate or combine the most relevant elements of each model in order to individualize treatment for substance abuse. Conversely stated, clinical work may be compromised by rigid adherence to any one model at all times for all patients, because each of the models has distinct disadvantages as well as advantages when applied to treatment. Different patients may benefit by emphasizing one model over another (Kissin, 1977). Likewise, the same patient may benefit by emphasizing different models during different phases of treatment. Thus, the critical question for treatment providers is how to match substance abusers during their treatment course to the various models in order to maximize treatment outcome (Glaser, 1980; Marlatt, 1988).

TABLE 2

Basic Models of Chemical Dependency

	Model				
	Moral	Learning	Disease	Self-Medication	Social
Etiology	Moral weakness lack of willpower; bad or evil character	Learned, maladaptive habits	Ideopathic; biological factors important	Symptom of another primary mental disorder	Environmental-Influences
Treatment Goal	Increased will-power against evil temptations	Self control via new learning	Complete abstinence to arrest disease progression	Improved mental functioning	Improved social functioning
Treatment Strategy	Religious counseling or conversion: punishment	Teaching of new coping skills and cognitive restructuring	Focus on chemical dependency as primary problem; reinforce identity as recovering alcoholic/addict	Psychotherapy and/ or pharmacotherapy of causative mental disorders	Altering of environment or coping responses to it
Advantages	Moral inventory and amends beneficial; holds users responsible for consequences; gauges counter-transference	Neither blaming nor punitive; emphasizes new learning; holds users responsible for new learning	Neither blaming nor punitive; disease implies treatment-seeking as appropriate response; does not focus on hypothetical etiologies	Neither blaming nor punitive emphasizes the importance of diagnosing and treating coexisting mental disorders	Emphasizes need for social supports and skills; easily integrated into other models
Disadvantages	Blaming and punitive; will-power ineffective	Undue emphasis on control	Underestimates co-existing mental disorders; cannot explain return to asymptomatic drinking	Implies that treatment of mental disorder is sufficient	Facilitates projection of blame; implies treatment of social problems is sufficient

Permission to reprint granted by source: Journal of Substance Abuse Treatment, Vol 6. pp. 147-157. 1989

The matching process will be seen to require an assessment of both the substance abuser's and the therapist's beliefs about treatment models. Moreover, proper assessment requires the clinician to view the substance abuser from the various perspectives offered by the various models (Shaffer, 1986a).

The five basic models will be discussed, then the dual diagnosis model presented, both as an example of an integrative model and as an example of treatment matching on the basis of beliefs.

Moral Model

The moral model of chemical dependency, historically, is the oldest. A recent Supreme Court decision in which alcoholism was interpreted as resulting from "willful misconduct," however, demonstrates that the moral model is still current and operative (Seessel, 1988). The characteristics of the moral model are presented in Table 3. In this model, chemical dependency results from a moral weakness or lack of willpower. The substance abuser is viewed as someone with a weak, bad or evil character. Accordingly, the goal of rehabilitation is to increase one's willpower in order to resist the evil temptation of substances. The user is expected to change from evil to good and from weak to strong. The strategies for change include both a "positive" reliance on God through religious counseling or conversion and a "negative" avoidance of punishment through criminal sanctions or damnation.

The major treatment disadvantage of the moral model is that it places the helping professional in an antagonist relationship with the substance abuser by adopting a judgmental stance that is blaming and punitive. The substance abuser is at fault in this model. If he or she does not change, then punishment is deserved. These attitudes are generally countertherapeutic. The other major disadvantage for treatment is that willpower for many, if not most substance abusers seen in treatment settings, is ineffective against chemical dependency. Although we are all well aware of histories in which alcoholic persons made a decision to quit and did so on their own, most individuals seen in treatment centers have already tried will power with little success. Therefore, a treatment strategy that depends solely on will power, sets the stage for failure and decreases a substance abuser's sense of self-esteem.

The moral model is often embraced by patients themselves who enter treatment feeling that they are bad and weak-willed. As a result, some patients ask for our help to make them strong enough to resist substances Once they feel strong enough, however, they can easily reason that they are strong enough to use substances again. A treatment goal of strength, therefore, can paradoxically lead to relapse. This is why Alcoholics Anonymous (A.A.) and other twelve step programs stress the concept of powerlessness over the substance. Nevertheless, it is important to determine which model the patient believes in.

Despite the disadvantages of the moral model, it focuses attention on the importance of moral concerns during the process of recovery for some substance abusers. A.A. for example, has long recognized that making a moral inventory of wrong-doing, coupled with making amends when possible, can be beneficial for recovery (Alcoholics Anonymous, 1976). In fact, steps 4 through 10, constituting over half of A.A.'s twelve steps, are devoted to moral concerns, even though A.A. ostensibly subscribes to the disease model of alcoholism. Three important points can be made here. First, A.A. is an example of an integrative approach, by combining elements of both the moral and disease models. Second, A.A. does not emphasize the moral elements of its program until step 4, exemplifying the principle of emphasizing different models during different phases of recovery. Third, A.A. and other twelve step programs actually refer to themselves as spiritual, rather than moral programs.

However, the spiritual model can be considered a variant of the moral model. It attributes chemical dependency to the substance abuser's misalliance with God and the universe. The substance abuser is viewed as someone who is alienated from God, stubbornly self-willed, and who attempts to dominate and control the outside world. Accordingly, the goal of treatment is to help substance abusers develop their spirituality by discovering and following God's will and by seeking a more "complementary" relationship with the universe (Brown, 1985).

Another treatment advantage of the moral model is that it holds people responsible for the consequences of their substance use. Although blaming people for having chemical dependency is seen as a disadvantage, holding people responsible for consequences is useful in overcoming denial and increasing motivation for change. Protecting substance abusers from the consequences of their use often "enables" them to continue using.

Finally, the moral model can be used as an advantage by clinicians in order to gauge the status of their treatment relationships with substance abusers and even to screen for psychopathology. We have all had the experience of finding ourselves in an antagonistic relationship with a substance abuser, feeling angry, blaming him or her for lack of motivation, and pushing for an administrative discharge from the treatment program. This experience should serve as a signal that we are operating under the moral model, regardless of our consciously espoused treatment model. The wise clinician will then ask why he or she has shifted to the moral model. One reason may be diagnosis. Substance abusers with an antisocial personality disorder, for example, really do have "bad characteristics" in addition to chemical dependency. Clinicians naturally respond to our perceptions of badness with moral model in terms of our treatment responses. By monitoring our treatment responses for their congruence with the various models of chemical dependency, we can gain important diagnostic information and be vigilant to our countertransference. Once aware of our countertransference, a psychiatric consultation for the substance abuser can be obtained and treatment more specifically designed for the antisocial personality, if present, can be recommended (Woody, McLellan, Luborsky, and O'Brien, 1985).

Learning Model

According to the learning model, chemical dependency and other addictive behaviors result from the learning of maladaptive habits (Marlatt, 1985a). The substance abuser is viewed as someone who learned "bad" habits through no particular fault of his or her own. Accordingly, the general goal of therapy is to teach new behaviors and cognitions that allow old habits to be controlled by new learning (see Table 2). Whether the specific goal of therapy is "controlled drinking" (to use alcohol as the example) or complete abstinence, the emphasis is on self-control. In this model, a "relapse" can be thought of as a loss of self-control resulting in harmful use of substances. The user is expected to change from a miseducated creature of maladaptive habits to a re-educated individual capable of self-control. The major strategy for change is education, including the teaching of new coping skills and cognitive restructuring (Marlatt, 1985a).

The salient advantages of the learning model are that it is neither punitive nor blaming for the development of maladaptive habits and that it stresses new learning and education as a treatment strategy. All legitimate treatment approaches value new learning, whether in the form of lectures, skills training, conditioning techniques, or psychotherapy. Another advantage of the learning model, like the moral model, is that it holds people responsible for obtaining and implementing the new learning (Marlatt, 1985a).

The prominent disadvantage is its emphasis on control. This disadvantage is not related to the controversy surrounding controlled drinking (Miller, 1983), because the learning model allows flexibility in choosing a treatment goal of either complete abstinence or controlled substance use. However, the model's emphasis on control ignores (a) the complex and hidden meanings this word can have for the substance abuser and (b) the therapeutic value for many substance abusers in admitting their loss of control. When a substance abuser and therapist agree that the goal of treatment will be self-control, even for the purpose of abstinence, the substance abuser may harbor a hidden goal based on the fantasy that one day the use of chemicals will be possible again once self-control is established. In this way, a treatment agreement for self-control may foster collusion with the substance abuser's denial of the need for abstinence. Alternatively, some substance abusers recover very well by internalizing the belief that they cannot control their chemical use and, therefore, that they cannot use chemicals. (The belief in loss of control is also stated in step 1 of A.A. as, "We admitted we were powerless over alcohol and that our lives had become unmanageable.") Therapists need to be aware that for some substance abusers, the concept of control is paradoxical; that is, in order to gain control, they must admit their loss of control (Brown, 1985). Therapists who can appreciate this paradox of control are in the best position to integrate, as needed, the models that emphasize loss of control with models that emphasize self-control. Indeed, the practical techniques of relapse prevention, which are based on a learning model of self-control (Marlatt, 1985a), are paradoxically utilized by many disease model programs that are based on the concepts of powerlessness and loss of control.

Disease Model

The disease model of alcoholism and other chemical dependencies is probably the dominant model among specialized treatment providers at present. Alcoholism as a disease, for example, has been officially endorsed by the American Medical Association, the American Psychiatric Association, the National Association of Social Workers, the World Health Organization, the American Public Health Association, and the National Council on Alcoholism (Clinical Social Work Journal, Volume 23, No. 3, 1995). According to this mode, the etiology of chemical dependency is unknown, but genetic and other biological factors are considered important (Schuckit, 1985). The substance abuser is viewed as someone who is ill or unhealthy, not because of an underlying mental disorder, but because of the disease of chemical dependency itself. The *sine qua non* of the disease is considered to be an irreversible loss of control over alcohol (Alcoholics Anonymous, 1976) or other substances. Once present, the disease is regarded as always present, because there is no known cure. Accordingly, the goal of treatment is complete abstinence. Without complete abstinence, the disease is regarded as progressive and often fatal. The user is expected to change from using to not using, from ill to healthy, and from unrecovered to recovering. The major treatment strategy is to focus on chemical dependency as the primary problem, rather than on lack of willpower, lack of self-control, or lack of mental health. The substance abuser is guided to develop a positive identification as a recovering alcoholic or addict who is powerless over substances. In addition, most disease model programs (as with the learning model) teach new behaviors to substitute for the substance use (such as going to A.A.), while family education and therapy are directed to eliminate "enabling" by significant others.

The advantages of the disease model are that it is neither punitive nor blaming and that it implies the importance of seeking treatment and help, as one would with any other disease. Guilt is alleviated because people are not held responsible for developing chemical dependency any more than for developing high blood pressure or diabetes. Blame can be directed towards the disease rather than towards the person with the disease. On the other hand, having a disease implies a responsibility for taking care of oneself by seeking treatment. In contrast to the learning model, the disease model emphasizes self-care rather than self-control. Another advantage is its clear focus on the chemical dependency as a problem to be treated in its own right. This focus prevents the dangers inherent in other models that focus primarily on postulated etiologies.

One disadvantage of the disease model is that it fails to account for those alcoholics who actually return to asymptomatic drinking (Shaffer, 1986b). The proportion of alcoholics who return to asymptomatic drinking has been estimated on the basis of a number of studies to be about 5 to 15% (Miller, 1983; Vaillant, 1983). These alcoholics tended to be less dependent on alcohol in terms of symptoms and duration, younger in age, and did not regard themselves as having a disease (Miller, 1983; Vaillant, 1983). Miller (1983) has even argued that these alcoholics were more likely to relapse when exposed to abstinence-oriented disease models, although only one study is cited to support that conclusion (Polich, Armor, & Braiker, 1981). Certainly, more research is needed to determine which alcoholics do best with which treatments because rigid adherence to one model for all alcoholics may be detrimental to some.

The other major disadvantage of the disease model is that some of its proponents fail to appreciate the possible independence of coexisting psychopathology. Many, if not most alcoholics, for example, experience depressive symptoms during the first year of abstinence (Schuckit, 1986). Brown (1985) has concluded that "the high percentage of respondents reporting depression suggests that it may be a necessary part of recovery". Unfortunately, the tendency to normalize depressive symptoms during early recovery by attributing them to the disease of alcoholism may inhibit efforts to diagnose and treat a coexisting "major depression" as defined by DSM-III-R

(American Psychiatric Association, 1987). Waiting through the first year of alcoholism treatment to allow symptoms of major depression to subside may work, but is unnecessarily cruel and potentially dangerous. The reason that it may work is because untreated major depressive episodes typically last about 6 months to 1 year (Kaplan & Sadock, 1988, p. 295). The reason that it is cruel is because major depression is responsive to appropriate pharmacotherapy within 4-6 weeks (Brotman, Falk, & Gelenberg, 1987). Regarding dangerousness, major depression is an unusually painful psychic state that can cause significant psychosocial disruption, if not relapse and suicide.

In contrast to the disease model, which tends to minimize coexisting psychopathology such as depression, the self-medication model primarily focuses on the psychopathology of substance abusers.

Self-Medication Model

According to this model, chemical dependency occurs either as a symptom of another primary mental disorder or as a coping mechanism for deficits in psychological structure or functioning (Khantzian, 1985). The substance abuser is viewed as someone who uses chemicals as a way to alleviate the painful symptoms of another mental disorder such as depression, or as a way to fill the void left by deficiencies in psychological structure or functioning. Consequently, the goal of treatment is to improve mental functioning. The user is expected to change from mentally ill to psychologically healthy. The strategies for change include psychotherapy and pharmacotherapy of the underlying mental disorder (see Table 3).

Like the learning and disease models, the self-medication model is neither punitive nor blaming. Another major advantage is that it stresses the importance of diagnosing and treating coexisting psychiatric problems when present. The importance of this is highlighted by treatment outcome studies that reveal different (usually worse) prognoses for addicts with additional psychopathology who enter traditional chemical dependency treatment programs (McLellan, Luborsky, Woody, O'Brien, & Druley, 1983; Rounsaville, Dolinsky, Babor, & Meyer, 1987).

The major disadvantage of this model stems from its emphasis on psychopathology as etiology. Although retrospective studies provide support for the idea that psychopathology causes chemical dependency, prospective studies do not (Vaillant, 1983). In many cases, psychopathology is the result, not the cause, of chemical dependency. In other cases, it is difficult to determine what is cause and what is effect when chemical dependency coexists with other psychopathology (Schuckit, 1986). Nevertheless, psychopathology may still be the cause of chemical dependency in some individuals. However, it does not necessarily follow that treating the cause in these individuals will provide sufficient treatment for the chemical dependency. This is because perpetuating factors of chemical dependency may develop in addition to the psychopathology that initiated the dependency (Brower, 1988). Optimal treatment, therefore, requires attention to both the initiating and perpetuating factors of substance abuse.

Unfortunately, the model implies that treatment of initiating psychiatric problems will provide sufficient treatment for chemical dependency. Therapists and substance abusers alike can easily believe that once the underlying cause is discovered and treated, then the problem with chemicals will disappear. For the substance abuser, postulating a treatable etiology allows for the hope that chemical use will one day be possible once the underlying cause is treated.

For the therapist, focusing treatment on underlying psychological factors can facilitate collusion with the substance abuser's denial of chemical dependency. The problem of colluding with denial can be highlighted by examining the various configurations of denial commonly encountered in substance abusers (Table 2). The four configurations listed depend on whether the denial is directed towards the chemical dependency, towards associated problems, towards both, or neither. Substance abusers who are in complete denial recognize neither their chemical dependency nor their other problems. They often have character disorders whose symptoms are ego-syntonic and disturbing to others but not themselves. They tend not to seek treatment unless forced by external pressures. Through the use of projection, they generally see others as having the problem rather than themselves. Substance abusers without character disorders may also adopt this configuration at times, especially when feeling threatened. Clearly, this configuration is difficult to treat and has resulted in the commonly heard clinical imperative to "break through the denial."

However, the other extreme is represented by those substance abusers who present no denial. These substance abusers are often suicidal because they are painfully aware of their chemical dependency, of the many conflicts -- about work or unemployment, with family, with the law -- and of the medical sequelae of their chemical dependency. Despite the clinical imperative to "break through" denial, this configuration is not recommended because substance abusers are at high risk for completed suicide, especially when feeling the full impact of their interpersonal losses and conflicts (Murphy, 1988).

It is the configuration of partial denial, Type 1 that poses the greatest challenge to the self-medication model. These substance abusers have denial for their chemical dependency but not for their other problems. Accordingly, they may seek treatment for their other problems such as depression, stress on the job, or interpersonal conflicts. If in the course of their evaluation or treatment, the therapist becomes aware of their harmful chemical use but adheres to the self-medication model, then collusion with the substance abuser's denial could occur. By covert agreement, the substance abuser and therapist will exclude the chemical dependency as an important focus of treatment. In effect, the substance abuser will be supported for focusing on the other problems, and the chemical use, if it is explored at all, will be interpreted as a coping mechanism. The disadvantage is that the substance abuser, significant others, and therapist will all have the illusion of treatment while the substance abuse continues.

The preferable configuration, at least for the initial stages of treatment, is the configuration of partial denial, Type 2. In this configuration, the substance abuser is encouraged to focus on the chemical dependency while denying or minimizing the significance of other problems. Rather than breaking through or eliminating denial, the therapist acts to redirect the denial away from the chemical dependency and towards the other problems (Wallace, 1978). When appropriate, the other problems can be interpreted as consequences of the chemical dependency. In addition, the substance abuser is presented with the rationale that the other problems are more likely to improve if the chemical dependency is treated first and that a period of abstinence is required in order to better assess the other problems.

TABLE 3
Configurations of Denial in Substance Abusers

Configuration	Chemical Dependency	Other Problems
Complete denial	I am not an alcoholic or addict	I have no other problems
No denial	I am an alcoholic and/or addict	I have all these other problems
Partial Denial (Type 1)	I am not an alcoholic or addict	Its just that I have all these other problems
Partial Denial (Type 2)	I am an alcoholic and/or addict	All my other problems are related to my substance use.

Permission to reprint granted by source: Journal of Substance Abuse Treatment, Vol. 6, pp. 147-157, 1989

Social Model

In this model, chemical dependency results from environmental, cultural, social, peer, or family influences (Beigel & Ghertner, 1977). The substance abuser is viewed as a product of external forces such as poverty, drug availability, peer pressure, and family dysfunction. Accordingly, the goal of treatment is to improve the social functioning of substance abusers by altering either their social environment or their coping responses to environmental stresses (see Table 2). In other words, users are expected to change either their environments or their coping responses. The strategies for changing the environment include family or couples therapy, attendance at self-help groups where one is surrounded by non-users, residential treatment, and avoidance of stressful environments where substances are readily available. The strategies for changing substance abusers' coping responses include group therapy, interpersonal therapy (Rounsaville, Gawin, & Kleber, 1985), social skills or assertiveness training, and stress management.

The major advantages of this model are its emphases on interpersonal functioning, social supports, environmental stressors, social pressures, and cultural factors as critical elements to address in treatment. The importance of addressing interpersonal functioning is underscored by data indicating that over one-half of alcoholic relapses are attributable to interpersonal conflicts (Marlatt, 1985b). Treatment interventions for alcoholics that are directed towards increasing social skills or environmental support have been shown to produce better outcomes 6-12 months after treatment (Eriksen, Bjornstad, & Gotestam, 1986; Page & Badgett, 1984). In general, treatment studies have consistently revealed better outcomes for alcoholics who are more socially stable, although the effect is strongest in short-term studies (Vaillant, 1983).

Cultures that introduce children to the ritualized use of low-proof alcohol during meals with others, discourage drinking at other times, and discourage drunkenness, have lower rates of alcoholism (Vaillant, 1983). In short, cultures that teach their children how to drink responsibly have lower rates of alcoholism, a conclusion which is also consistent with the learning model. While this conclusion has greater ramifications for primary prevention than for treatment of alcoholism, other cultural factors such as ethnicity and the socialization of women may have important implications for those entering treatment. Treatment programs which are "culturally sensitive" to ethnicity and to women's social roles may produce better outcomes for specific ethnic groups and for women, although treatment outcome studies that specifically address this issue are unfortunately lacking (Amaro, Beckman, & Mays 1987; Reed 1987).

Another advantage of the social model is that it is readily compatible with, and easily integrated into, other models. Here are three examples: First, the learning model encourages both the enlistment of social support during treatment (Marlatt, 1985c) and the teaching of alternative coping responses to environmental stresses and interpersonal conflicts (Marlatt, 1985a). Indeed, the learning model is sometimes referred to as the social-learning model, because learning describes a process that occurs in an environmental and interpersonal context. In other words, people learn from their experiences with their environment and with other people. Second, the self-medication model conceptualizes substance abuse as a way of coping with psychological deficits resulting from frustrating and damaging relationships during early development (Khantzian, 1985). In this model, individual psycho-dynamic psychotherapy is viewed as a primary treatment (Khantzian, 1984) that focuses on relationships with other people in terms of the transference relationships that develop with the therapist (Kohut, 1971; Schiffer, 1988). Third, many proponents of the disease model view the entire family as both affected by the disease and suffering from the parallel "disease" of codependency (Cermak, 1986). Treatment is aimed at helping the family embark on its own recovery. Thus, most of the other models incorporate the social model to some extent in their treatment approaches, and they also regard improved social functioning as an important measure of successful treatment outcome. Conversely, there seems to be a disadvantage in using the social model as an exclusive treatment mode because the etiology of substance abuse is multifactorial, implying a need for multiplp treatment strategies (Donovan, 1986; Kissin, 1977).

The major treatment disadvantage of the social model is that it may facilitate projection of blame onto others and the environment. The substance abuser may come to feel victimized by others or by circumstances that do not seem changeable and thus renounce responsibility for solutions. Substance abusers who see themselves as victims require the therapist's emphatic guidance towards taking an active role in changing their environment or their coping responses to it. The substance abuser is similarly guided by the Serenity Prayer of A.A. which encourages each person "to accept the things I cannot change," by learning to cope with them, and "to change the things I can."

A related disadvantage of the social model occurs when the therapist focuses exclusively on social problems, while minimizing the chemical dependency itself. Substance abusers, for example, may seek treatment for problems with their marriage or job. The therapist's questions about substance use during early interviews may be met with statements such as "I drink because my job is stressful" or "You would use drugs too if you were married to my spouse." Such statements represent rationalizations and projections that are expressed in the form of beliefs in the social model. The substance abuser with these complaints may tempt the inexperienced therapist, who also endorses the social model, to focus on job or marital problems, while mutually denying the importance of the substance abuse problem. This disadvantage was described above in terms of the Type 1 partial denial configuration.

Dual Diagnosis Model

Substance abusers who present, with depression or social problems are commonly encountered, as discussed earlier. Some of these individuals will insist that their depression or other problems should be the focus of treatment, rather than their substance abuse. Their belief is in either the self-medication model or the social model. Many substance abusers might complain primarily of depression, while minimizing their substance abuse. These are substance abusers who believe in the self-medication model. Essentially, they state that they use substances because they are depressed. Their treatment will depend on the beliefs of their therapists.

If the therapist also believes in the self-medication model, then treatment will focus primarily on the depression. The potential pitfall here is a treatment match based on collusion (see Table 5), in which both the therapist and substance abuser believe in depression as a focus of treatment but mutually deny the importance of substance abuse. By contrast, if the therapist believes in the disease model, then statements such as "I use substances because I am depressed" are interpreted as rationalizations. Substance abusers may become defensive when their use of substances is explored. The therapeutic task is then formulated by the disease model therapist in terms of breaking through the defensiveness and denial. The potential pitfall here is a mismatch of beliefs resulting in an antagonistic relationship, instead of an alliance in which treatment can occur (Table 4.).

TABLE 4
Typology of Treatment Matches

Type of Match	Therapist and Substance Abuser	Treatment Effect
Match	Believe in same model	Variable
Collusion	Mutually deny problems that do not fit model	Countertherapeutic
Alliance	All problems addressed over time	Therapeutic
Mismatch	Do not believe in same model	Countertherapeutic unless mismatch is addressed and resolved

Permission to reprint granted by source: Journal of Substance Abuse Treatment, Vol. 6, pp 147-157, 1989

The way out of this clinical dilemma is first to assess carefully everyone's beliefs in order to guard against either collusion or a mismatch, both of which are countertherapeutic. Next, the substance abuser is invited into an alliance without collusion by the following intervention: "I agree that you appear depressed and this is certainly a problem for you. We need to address that. It is also true from what you have told me that you have a diagnosis of chemical dependency. We need to address that too and let me tell you why. Any attempt I make to determine the type of depression you have will be confounded by further chemical use. Also, any treatment that I can give you for your depression will be sabotaged by further chemical use. This is because we know that regardless of which came first (the depression or the chemicals) and regardless of why you use, chemicals make depression worse over long periods of time. In short, you have two problems, they both require treatment, and the best way to treat your depression right now is to give you treatment for chemical dependency. After that treatment is begun, we will be better able to see if other treatments for your depression are needed."

In essence, the substance abuser is invited to believe in the dual diagnosis model (see Table 5) in which the argument about what is the primary problem requiring treatment is replaced by the idea that treatment is required for both problems. In this way, the therapist and substance abuser can build an alliance around a common goal, which is to treat depression, without denying the importance of treating chemical dependency.

Like the self-medication model, the dual diagnosis model views the coexisting mental disorder as a primary problem that may require its own psychotherapeutic or pharmacotherapeutic intervention. This helps to build an alliance with the substance abuser and prevents the minimization of coexisting mental disorders by the therapist. Like the disease model, the dual diagnosis model also views substance abuse as a primary problem requiring its own treatment. This helps to prevent collusion with the substance abuser and insures that the importance of substance abuse treatment will not be overlooked. Properly applied, the dual diagnosis model integrates elements of both the self-medication and disease models in a way that avoids the disadvantages of adhering to only one or the other.

In the dual diagnosis model, substance abuse and other mental disorders can be seen as coexisting without necessarily attributing one etiologically to the other. Both are considered primary disorders that can exacerbate one another. The strategy for treatment is to focus on both disorders, although substance use must first stop in order to diagnose and treat the coexisting mental disorder. If an initial period of abstinence proves to be sufficient treatment for coexisting mental disorder, then a shift from the dual diagnosis model toward other models can be made, as appropriate.

When both the therapist and substance abuser believe in a common explanatory system that does not deny important problems requiring treatment, then a treatment match based on a healthy alliance has been achieved (Table 5). Obviously, this type of match is preferred, but cannot be expected to occur by accident. Only by carefully monitoring our own beliefs and those of the substance abusers receiving treatment, can this type of match be achieved. Furthermore, substance abusers may require the use of integrative models in order to establish a therapeutic alliance. Therefore, integrative models may provide the optimal clinical strategy for bridging discrepant belief systems between therapists and substance abusers.

TABLE 5

Models of Chemical Dependency and Co-existing Depression

Model	Primary Disorder	Secondary Relationship Disorder	Treatment Between Disorders	Treatment Strategy
Disease Model	Chemical Dependency	Depression	Depression = withdrawal symptom, response to losses due to chemical use, or physiological response to chemical	Treat chemical dependency, depression will remit
Self-Medication Model	Depression	Chemical Dependency	Chemical Dependency= symptom of depression, or coping response to depression and losses associated with depression	Treat depression, chemical dependency will remit
Dual Diagnosis Model	Both depression and chemical dependency	Neither	Each may exacerbate the other, but neither is a symptom of the other	Treat both

Permission to reprint granted by source: Journal of Substance Abuse Treatment Vol. 6, pp. 147-157, 1989

Dr. Michael Mullan

CHAPTER 4

CASE STUDY

The following case study project involves the treatment of an individual, known here as George J. (This is not the individuals true name). George was initially presented to treatment for chronic alcoholism. The patient was brought into the treatment facility by his parents. His parents stated that despite numerous treatment attempts, George had been unable to maintain any significant length of abstinence from alcohol. Prior to entering treatment George had been treated at a local hospital for injuries sustained when he drove his bicycle over an embankment, while intoxicated. His parents stated that George had been in the ditch overnight, and that he was found the following morning by a passing pedestrian. George was treated at a local hospital for his immediate medical conditions. After George's stabilization, the hospital recommended that he be referred to a treatment center for his alcoholism. During the initial intake screening process, George stated that he was a forty-two year old medical doctor who had been unable to practice medicine for the past three years due in part, to his alcoholism. George stated that he had had four previous treatment episodes for his alcoholism. He had been hospitalized two times in 1993, once in 1994, and once in 1995. The patient stated that he had also been hospitalized in a psychiatric hospital in 1993 for a period of ten days, following a failed suicide attempt. At that time, George had been given two DSM IV Axis I Diagnostic codes -- Axis-I 303.90 - Alcoholism, and 296.3x - Major Depression recurrent. Upon admission into detox George had been prescribed Librium as a preventative measure to offset any adverse detoxification consequences that might occur, such as Delirium Tremors (DT's) or seizures. These events can occur when a chronic alcoholic such as George, abruptly stops the intake of alcohol. The Librium was prescribed on a step down basis.

<u>Step Down</u>

Day 1	25 mg	Four times per day
Day 2	25 mg	Four times per day
Day 3	25 mg	Four times per day
Day 4	25 mg	Three times per day
Day 5	25 mg	Three times per day
Day 6	25 mg	Three times per day
Day 7	25 mg	Two times per day
Day 8	25 mg	Two times per day
Day 9	25 mg	One time per day
Day 10	25 mg	One time per day

George had also been prescribed Doxepin in 1993 for his depression, however, George stated that he had only taken the medication on an intermittent basis. Due to this fact it was determined by the facility M.D., Dr. Kenneth Hart, that George had never gained the full beneficial effects of the medication. Dr. Hart felt that it would be in George's best interest to discontinue the Doxepin in the initial stages of his treatment. George was then to be re-evaluated at a later date to determine if his depression was a result of his alcoholism in which case the depression should clear. If the depression did not subside medication would be prescribed at that time.

An effective treatment approach was required in order to deal with George's specific needs. Because George had two separate Axis I Diagnosis', and numerous failed treatment experiences, the theoretical approach selected for this case study was the Integrative Dual Diagnosis Treatment approach.

Integrative Dual Diagnosis Treatment Approach

George received his treatment at Cedar House Rehabilitation Center (CHRC). Which uses the 12-step program approach as its basic framework, while integrating aspects of various other theoretical approaches. Such as the use of Psychotropic medications when indicated, individual and group therapy sessions and family participation whenever possible. The following is a description of CHRC's Dual Disorder Program. The program was used as the framework for George's treatment experience.

Program Description

Cedar House Rehabilitation Center (CHRC) is a 125-bed residential facility located in Southern California. The program offers various levels of care, i.e. residential treatment, day treatment, outpatient, and sober living. CHRC is unique to the area served because of the dual disorder component of the program. This program services approximately 20% of the total population at any given time. Upon initial intake clients are screened, and placed in the appropriate treatment component that will match their individual needs and enhance their treatment experience.

Because George fit the criteria for the Dual Disorder component, the client was matched to this program. The length of stay in this program varies from 30 to 90 days. Average length of stay is 60 days. After the clients complete the intensive inpatient component, they are often referred to the outpatient program for an additional six months, or they are referred back to their respective private, or county mental health providers for ongoing care.

Policy and Procedure For Dual Disorder Clients

A.) PROGRAM DESCRIPTION

The purpose of the Dual Disorders Treatment Program (DDTP) is to provide comprehensive services to meet the needs of individuals with coexisting mental disorders and addiction to alcohol and/or other drugs (AOD Use Disorders). Psychiatric disorders and AOD Use Disorders can and do coexist: one disorder may precipitate the emergence of the other, or the two disorders may occur independently of each other. Determining whether the disorders are related may be difficult, and may not be of great significance with an individual like George who has had a history of longstanding combined disorders.

The failure to adequately assess and treat coexisting mental illness along with AOD Use Disorders has long been associated with AOD Disorder relapse and/or decompensation with a psychiatric disorder in many cases.

The behaviors seen in some psychiatric disorders can mimic behaviors associated with AOD abuse and dependence problems. Since some of the dysfunctional and maladaptive behaviors that are consistent with AOD abuse and dependence may have other causes, such as physical, psychological and/or social problems, a multidisciplinary approach is used in the assessment and treatment of persons with possible dual disorders. The use of varied assessment tools, to include a thorough psychosocial assessment, history of prior psychiatric disturbance and treatment, family history of psychiatric and/or chemical dependency disorders, corroborating information from family and others, along with drug testing, is critical to confirm AOD and/or psychiatric disorders. This process will be described in detail in the assessment section below.

In addition to the issues of adequate diagnostic assessment, the level of functioning of each dual disordered person must be assessed. The symptoms of co-occurring psychiatric disorder may be misinterpreted as poor or incomplete "recovery" from AOD addiction. Psychiatric disorders may interfere with the client's ability and motivation to participate in addiction treatment, as well as their compliance with treatment guidelines. Therefore, it is necessary to develop and implement flexible, individualized treatment plans and objectives to meet each client's specific needs while maximizing their capabilities. It is important to ascertain whether each client is capable of benefiting from the treatment program available at the

Cedar House Rehabilitation Center, or whether referral for another level of care is warranted.

The primary goals of the Dual Disorders Program are to optimize the functioning and quality of life for each program participant.

B.) TARGET POPULATION

The Dual Disorders Treatment Program is designed for adult men and women, 18 years and older, who are experiencing progressively deteriorating functioning in life as a result of abusing alcohol and/or other drugs, who meet specific dimensional admission criteria, and who have a coexisting mental illness as a secondary diagnosis. Such individuals often have demonstrated an impaired ability to function in employment, family and social relationships and other areas of life. These individuals may be unable to maintain abstinence from alcohol and other drugs without professional intervention. Since addictive disorder is thought of as a "Family Disease", family members and/or significant others attend group and individual therapy sessions two times per week while their family member is in treatment. These groups are facilitated by a Licensed Clinical Social Worker (LCSW), and Case Manager.

C.) ADMISSIONS CRITERIA

Admission into the Dual Disorders Treatment Program requires that the individual meet established criteria as defined in the Admissions Criteria, Policy No. PRG-008. (1) The client must be stabilized on any medications that they might be taking. (2) The client must be capable of participating in, and benefiting from the program. In addition, clients who are assessed as having a co-occurring psychiatric disorder, but who do not have an attending psychiatrist at the time of admission, may be referred for a concurrent psychiatric evaluation and treatment planning while they participate in the Cedar House Rehabilitation Center Program.

Clients will be further assessed for their functional ability to participate in the treatment program. Clients will be deemed appropriate for treatment in the program unless their impairments prevent them from adequately comprehending and attending to program activities, materials, and assignments. Clients must not pose a risk of harming themselves or others.

D.) TREATMENT PROCESS PROTOCOL

1.) IDENTIFICATION AND INITIAL ASSESSMENT PROCESS Clients will be identified for screening for the Dual Disorders Treatment Program using the following guidelines:

a.) Clients who are admitted to the Cedar House Rehabilitation Center with a previously diagnosed psychiatric disorder in addition to the AOD Use Disorder which precipitated admission.

b.) Clients who do not have a previous psychiatric diagnosis, who have been admitted to the primary program, and who are displaying unusual thinking or behavior patterns that might indicate the presence of a psychiatric disorder in addition to the AOD Use Disorder.

c.) Clients who have been identified as having a need for additional treatment for psychiatric problems per the

Addictions Severity Index which is administered on admission.

2.) SCREENING PROCEDURE

a.) Clients identified above as potential candidates for the Dual Disorders Treatment Program will be screened as follows:

1.) Each of these clients will be assigned to a counselor who is a member of the Dual Disorders Treatment Team (DDTT) and who will provide the initial assessment. This counselor will function as a case manager for the client throughout his/her treatment with CHRC to not only provide direct assessment and counseling services, but also to coordinate the development and delivery of other needed resources. Clients will be administered the SCID, which is a screening instrument for current psychiatric disturbance. The counselor will also provide a thorough psychosocial assessment, to include history of prior psychiatric disturbance and treatment, family history of psychiatric and/or chemical dependency disorders, and corroborating information from family and others. The facility Medical Director and Nurse will provide the medical examination and clearances according to existing policy. Each of these clients may be tested for recent

AOD use, and possibly be referred for detoxification, as needed.

2.) These clients will then be evaluated by a designated member of the DDTT under the direct supervision of a licensed mental health professional. The purpose of this evaluation is to assess possible mental illness and to ascertain the client's functional status. The licensed mental health professional member of the DDTT will be responsible for making the final determination of the existence of a mental illness. In the event of a finding of mental illness, and if the client does not already have an attending psychiatrist, the licensed mental health professional may make a recommendation that the client be evaluated by a psychiatrist for concurrence on the diagnosis and for medication management. If the client is already being seen by a psychiatrist, the appropriate releases of information will be executed to allow the DDTT to coordinate treatment planning and implementation.

b.) Upon completion of the initial assessment process the counselor will then begin formulation of an individualized treatment plan in consultation with the DDTT. Each client's assessment and treatment plan will be reviewed in a case conference supervised by the licensed mental health professional. In the initial case conference the DDTT will review the assessment information and formulate the initial treatment plans. Discharge criteria and exit planning will be incorporated into the treatment plan from the outset.

c.) The Medical Director will participate in a weekly review and approval of the assessments, treatment plans and progress reviews, and provide guidance as indicated.

3.) TREATMENT AND DISCHARGE PLANNING

a.) Clients admitted to the DDTP will be provided with specialized treatment plans that incorporate outcome goals related to amelioration of both the chemical dependency and the psychiatric problems.

b.) DDTP clients will be admitted to selected components of the long term chemical dependency treatment program to the extent that their level of functioning permits. In addition, these clients will be provided with specialized group and individual therapy designed to address their particular needs as identified in the assessment and treatment planning process.

c.) In subsequent weekly case conferences, the case manager will present the case to the DDTT to review progress in all identified problem areas, identify new problems as they arise, and amend the treatment plan as needed.

d.) Discharge Planning is essential in promoting long term recovery and optimal functioning in the community. In recognition of this fact, Discharge Planning is to be addressed from the onset as a discrete problem on the Master Problem List.

e.) Many DDTP clients will require referrals for specialized services to address impaired functioning in vocational, social, medical, psychological and other areas. In these cases, the counselor functions as a case manager in brokering the needed services and ensuring that the appropriate linkages are in place prior to the client's exit from residential treatment.

f.) Whenever it may be indicated, the DDTP will provide a continuum of care such that clients may be treated in residential, day treatment, or outpatient settings, and concurrently participate in outside support groups, and/or other treatment with mental health or other providers.

E.) PROGRAM EVALUATION AND REVIEW

The DDTP will develop and process outcome criteria which will serve to provide objective measures of the program's effectiveness in meeting it's stated goals. These measures will ensure that the program has the requisite information to meet needed quality assurance guidelines.

F.) DUAL DISORDERS TREATMENT TEAM

The DDTP consists of the Medical Director, Clinical Director, Program Director, or their designees, the Clinical Consultant, The Nurse, and designated counseling/case management and station staff.

In addition to the regularly scheduled case conference meetings, the DDTT may be convened for conferring about a particularly difficult client on an ad hoc basis. The DDTT will also meet regularly with the Program Director to review the program, address any problems that are identified, and make changes to enhance the program's meeting it's objectives, as needed.

Integrative Treatment Approach

The first step in the Treatment Planning process is to obtain as much history from the client as possible. This was done in George's case with the use of a comprehensive Psycho Social evaluation. From information gathered in this evaluation effective individualized treatment planning and matching could be determined.

The following is a summary of George J.'s Psycho Social evaluation:

Client is a 42-year-old divorced white male. Client has two minor children. One son - age 9, one daughter - age 4. Both children reside with client's ex-wife in Seattle. Client is currently unemployed from his profession as a Medical Doctor (M.D.). Client states that he has been unable to practice medicine for the past two years due to his alcoholism. Client states no income at this time. Client states that he has been living with his parents for the past six months. Both parents are recovering alcoholics who attend A.A. Client's father is a retired Psychologist who has been sober for 14 years. Client's mother is a retired School Teacher who has been in recovery for 15 years. Client is the oldest of three children. He states he has two younger sisters. Client states that the middle child has been in recovery for two years, and his youngest sister is a social drinker. Client states that his family would be willing to participate in his treatment. Client states his only medical complaint is a hernia and that it causes him a great deal of discomfort at this time. Client states he has been arrested three times - two times for Driving Under the Influence (DUI), and one time for Public Intoxication. His last arrest was two weeks ago for Driving Under the Influence. Client has Court case pending. Client has had four previous treatment episodes for his alcoholism. Client states that his longest period of sobriety was three months. Client states that he began to use alcohol at age 13 and that his drinking got out of control about five years ago. Client states that he goes on extended binges and that he consumes one to two fifths of Vodka daily. Client states a Psy history. Client was hospitalized in 1993 after a failed suicide attempt. Client was placed on Doxepin (100 mg. 1x daily) for treatment of his depression. Client states that he has not been taking the medication, and feels that he needs to be placed back on the medication. Client's current Psy function appear depressed, but otherwise stable. Upon intake client was given a Librium step down as a preventative measure. Client's motivating factor for treatment is his complete loss of control and feelings of hopelessness. Client states a strong desire for lasting sobriety. Client had good eye contact throughout the assessment process. Client wept openly on numerous occasions. Client's appearance was neat and clean. Client does appear to be in a great deal of emotional pain. I believe that it would be in client's best interest to be admitted to our Long Term Dual Disorder Program.

CASE STUDY
GEORGE J.- TREATMENT EXPERIENCE

Phase 1. Detoxification

Upon intake into the program George was placed in the detoxification unit for a 72-hour period, so George's condition could be closely monitored by the Center's medical staff. While in detoxification George's vital signs were checked on a regular basis, (i.e. pulse rate, blood pressure, and overall general physical status. George's detoxification from alcohol was moderate to severe. George showed signs of elevated blood pressure, and increased pulse rate. George also suffered erratic sleep patterns and stated that when he did sleep, he experienced extremely bad nightmares. Because of George's heavy drinking pattern, his physical deterioration, and his age, George was given a ten-day gradual step down of Librium.

Librium is often prescribed to severe/chronic alcoholics while they are going through the detoxification period, to prevent any adverse consequences, i.e. Delirium Tremors (DT's), seizures, or possibly even death. (Dr. Kenneth Hart, M.D., CHRC Medical Director).

Phase 2. Long Term Treatment, Assessment and Planning.

Upon George's completion of detoxification he was placed into CHRC's long term treatment program component. Subsequent to George's Psychosocial evaluation, a Master Problem List was identified.

MASTER PROBLEM LIST

1.) George's inability to refrain from the use of alcohol outside of a structured environment.
2.) Clinical Depression recurrent.
3.) Strained family relationships.
4.) Unresolved legal issue (pending court date - DUI).
5.) George's loss of job and suspension of his medical license.

After the identification of these five problem areas, five specific treatment plans were formulated to address each of these issues.

Treatment Plan 1

Problem No. 1

Inability to refrain from alcohol outside of a structured environment.

A.) It is the philosophy of CHRC that Alcoholism and Drug Addiction are each considered a disease. Therefore, a primary goal of treatment is to educate each client on the Disease Concept of alcoholism. George was asked to participate in all alcoholism education groups, lectures, and group therapies as facilitated by CHRC staff.

B.) Educate George in the 12-step program of Alcoholics Anonymous (A.A.) - A central theme of treatment at CHRC revolves around the 12-steps. George was asked to complete steps 1-5 of the A.A. program while in treatment.

FIRST FIVE STEPS OF A.A.

1.) We admitted we were powerless over alcohol, that our lives had become unmanageable.

In using a 12-step program it is believed that an alcoholic must first and foremost admit that he/she is powerless over their alcoholism, and that because of powerlessness (i.e. loss of control) that their lives have become unmanageable. This is often a very difficult concept for individuals such as George to accept. Doctors are trained to be in control. Yet George's life was very much out of control.

2.) Came to believe that a Power greater than ourselves could restore us to sanity.

This particular step serves two functions for the alcoholic. (1) That the alcoholic needs help, he/she cannot control his/her drinking alone; (2) Being restored to sanity implies that George's behavior while drinking was insane behavior, continued despite numerous adverse consequences.

3.) Made a decision to turn our will and our lives over to the care of God *as we understood Him.*

For many alcoholics such as George, this step is a very difficult to accept. It constitutes giving up control to a Power greater than oneself. The idea of a "Higher Power" is often foreign, or unacceptable to many alcoholics who have a difficult time with the concept of a Higher Power. These individuals will often use the group as their "Higher Power." Again, this step deals with powerlessness, and loss of control.

It is important that the alcoholic make a cognitive decision to reach out for help and begin to make positive changes.

4.) Made a searching and fearless moral inventory of ourselves.

5.) Admitted to God, to ourselves, and to another human being the exact nature of our wrongs.

Steps four and five can be extremely therapeutic in helping individuals to make an honest assessment of past behavior and to move forward with an honest realistic acceptance of self. These steps fit well with the Rogerian Theory. The primary objective of Rogerian therapy is to resolve an incongruence - to help clients become able to accept and be themselves. To this end, client-centered therapists establish a Psychological climate in which clients can feel free, unconditionally accepted, understood, and valued as people. In this climate they can begin to feel free, for perhaps the first time, to explore their real feelings and thoughts and to accept hates and angers and "ugly feelings" as part of themselves. As their self-concept becomes more congruent with their actual experiences, they become more self accepting and more open to new experiences and new perspectives. In short, they become better integrated people (Carl Rogers, 1966).

Problem No. 2:

Clinical Depression Recurrent

Goal: Stabilization of George's depression.

Method used to achieve this goal:

A.) Educate George on the problems associated with having a dual disorder.

    1.) Attend all dual disorder lectures, and dual disorder group therapies as facilitated by CHRC staff.

B.) Reinforce George's awareness of his Depressive Disorder.

    1.) George was re-evaluated following a 21-day period, to assess the level of his depression. It was determined at that time that his depression was ongoing, and had not subsided. George was then placed back on his medication, Doxepin 100mg. 1x daily.

Sinequan (Doxepin Hydrochloride) is one of a class of Psychotherapeutic agents known as Dibenzoxepin Tricyclic Components. Sinequan is recommended for treatment of:

1.) Psychoneurotic patients with depression and/or anxiety.

2.) Depression and/or anxiety associated with alcoholism (not to be taken concomitantly with alcohol).

3.) Depression and/or anxiety associated with organic disease (the possibility of drug interaction should be considered if the patient is receiving other drugs concomitantly).

4.) Psychotic depressive disorders with associated anxiety, including Involution Depression and manic-depressive disorders.

The target symptoms of Psychoneurosis that respond particularly well to Sinequan include anxiety, tension, depression, somatic symptoms and concerns, sleep disturbances, guilt, lack of energy, fear, apprehension and worry. Clinical experience has shown that Sinequan is safe and well-tolerated even in the elderly patient.

Medication Dosage and Administration

For most patients with illness of mild to moderate severity, a starting daily dose of 75mg. is recommended. Dosage may subsequently be increased or decreased at appropriate intervals and according to individual response. The usual optimum dose range is 75mg/day to 150mg/day.

In the case of more severely ill patients, higher doses may be required with subsequent gradual increase to 300mg/day, if necessary. Additional therapeutic effect is rarely to be obtained by exceeding a dose of 300mg/day. In conjunction with George's chemotherapy, George was assigned to a therapist for Psycotherapy. George was to see the therapist two times per week for the duration of his treatment.

Problem No. 3

Strained relationship with family.

Goal: Improve family relationships.

Method used to achieve this goal:

A.) The measures that were employed to achieve this goal were to invite George's mother and father to participate in George's recovery, i.e. Family Therapy. George's parents attended Family Group while George was in treatment.

The family component of CHRC is facilitated by a Licensed Clinical Social Worker (LCSW), and a Case Manager. This group meets two evenings per week. Family members and clients are given the opportunity to address issues relating to interpersonal conflicts caused by addiction. Because George's parents are both recovering alcoholics, and George grew up in an alcoholic home, it was determined that it would be essential to George's recovery have his family involved.

The Theory of Homeostasis

A common bond or thread runs through family members. Jackson (1957) coined the term "Family Homeostasis" to define a balancing behavior in families. "This balance of equilibrium shifts in response to changes which occur within the family (illness, aging, death, unemployment) and influential forces from without (economic, political, social)" (Meeks and Kelly, 1970, p. 400). Ewing and Fox (1968) adopted theoretical concepts from Jackson's theory of Homeostasis in Families. They view the alcoholic marriage as a "Homeostatic Mechanism" that is "Established to resist change over long periods of time. The behavior of each spouse is rigidly controlled by the other. As a result, an effort by one person to alter typical role behavior threatens the family equilibrium and provokes renewed efforts by the spouse to maintain status quo." Alcohol is often a key part in the balance of the alcoholic family.

Wegscheider (1981) explains that in the chemically dependent family each person is affected by the chemical abuse of one member and says that "In an attempt to maintain balance, members compulsively repress their feelings and develop survival behaviors and walls of defense to protect them from the pain."

Family balance is often achieved in the alcoholic family with drinking as a central point. When this drinking is removed through treatment, the family is thrown into turmoil as if it were a mobile in a windstorm. Mother is not needed as the overly responsible martyr when dad returns to take over running the household. Brother has no reason to stay away from home and must re-evaluate his relationship with dad. The family suddenly notices little sister's hyperactive mannerisms. The emotional distance of the marriage may still exist. Without family intervention, drinking may reoccur; the family may separate; or a new family member may become symptomatic.

This appeared to be the case in George's family. Both George and his middle sister became alcoholics, while the youngest sister by George's report, is considered to be a social drinker.

Family Constellation

With the addition of other children and the solidification of rules and roles, a family constellation develops. In the average family, some generalities can be made about birth order. First-born children are, for a while, only children. They compare themselves with adults and learn the rules of adult interaction, sometimes becoming pseudoadults. The second-born children come along and dethrone the first born, and competition is set up. When the third-born children arrive, they turn the second born into middle children, who often become occupied with making sure things are fair.

The youngest child is usually looked upon as the baby and may act cute, weak, or awkward. The youngest child may demand service or act like the family clown. These birth order roles play a part in determining what survival behavior each child adopts to maintain homeostasis when a family becomes dysfunctional. Lawson et al. (1983).

Because of the extensive substance abuse in George's family of origin, the treatment team felt that this would be one of the most critical issues to address if George were to maintain long term sobriety.

B.) Because George's minor children lived out-of-state, they were unable to participate in the family program component, however, George was encouraged to open lines of communication with his children through letters, and weekly telephone contact.

Problem No. 4

Unresolved legal issues.

Goal: Resolve legal issues.

Method used to achieve this goal:

A.) Because George had been arrested for his second Driving Under the Influence (DUI) offense just two weeks prior to entering treatment, George was asked to:

1.) Attend all mandated court appearances.

2.) Adhere to any orders from the court.

It was the consensus of the treatment team that unless George resolved these legal matters, his probability of successful abstinence would be greatly reduced.

Problem No. 5

George's loss of job, and suspension of his medical license.

Goal: Get George stabilized, and his medical license reinstated.

Method used to achieve this goal:

A.) George was asked to contact the State Medical Board, and take the necessary steps toward getting his medical license reinstated.

SUMMARY OF TREATMENT EXPERIENCE

George remained in the inpatient component of the program for 60 days and successfully completed that phase of treatment. He then relocated to a sober living environment and enrolled in the outpatient component of the program for a period of six months.

While in treatment, George completed steps 1-5 of the Alcoholics Anonymous program material as requested by the treatment team. He and his parents continued Family Therapy for six months of the outpatient program.

During the six-month period George opened lines of communication with his children. He visited them in Seattle, and continued reunification.

George made all his court appearances and due to his active, ongoing participation in CHRC's recovery program George was sentenced to three days in county jail, which he served. He was also placed on three years summary probation, and ordered to go through a drinking driver program.

George contacted the State Medical Board for reinstatement of his license to practice medicine. He was ordered to go through the Medical Board's Diversion Program, in which he is currently participating. The program is a highly structured 12-step based program. George is required to attend weekly meetings and is subject to random drug/alcohol testing. George has now remained abstinent (alcohol free) for the past year. I believe that his prognosis is excellent.

CHAPTER 5

DISCUSSION

The case study of George J. presented a number of problems that indicated the use of an integrative treatment approach.

First, George had experienced a number of multiple treatment failures. Second, George's alcoholism was pervasive and had affected almost every aspect of his life, (i.e. loss of family through divorce, loss of occupation, strained relations with his family of origin, and pending legal actions.) George had been given two Axis I Diagnosis', Alcoholism and Major Depression Recurrent, which lead to his hospitalization in 1993 after a failed suicide attempt.

When working with individuals who are dually disordered it is not unusual for them to have experienced multiple failed treatment experiences. One possible explanation for this is that many treatment facilities only address one disorder, and do not treat the other disorder. Many traditional treatment centers do not believe in the use of Psychotropic medications. Therefore, they only treat the alcoholism and in a case like George's, do not address the depression, or they might suggest that the depression will go away once the person stops drinking. This type of treatment will in all probability not work with someone who is truly dually disordered, and can ultimately be even more damaging when the person's depression reoccurs and they relapse back into drinking. They often times feel even worse about themselves, thinking that they are truly worthless human beings.

It is essential when working with dually disordered individuals that one keep an open mind. Treatment must be tailored to meet the individual needs of the patient.

In George's case, five separate theories were integrated. 1) The 12-step program of Alcoholics Anonymous; 2) Cognitive behavioral therapy, the conviction that congnitive process influence both motivation and behavior. The use of behavior changing techniques in therapy sessions that were like experiments in which the therapist and George applied learning principles to alter George's cognitions continuously evaluating the effects that changes in cognition have on both thoughts and outer behavior; 3) Ellis theory of Rational Emotive Therapy (RET) unfortunately many people have learned unrealistic beliefs and perfectionist values that cause them to expect too much of themselves, leading them to behave irrationally and then feel unnecessarily that they are worthless failures. For example, a person may think "I should be able to win everyone's love and approval" or "I should be thoroughly adequate and competent in everything I do." Such unrealistic assumptions and self-demands inevitably lead to ineffective and self-defeating behavior in the real world, which reacts accordingly, and then to the recognition of failure and the emotional response of self-evaluation. This emotional response is thus the necessary consequence not of "reality", but of the individual's faulty expectations, interpretations, and self-damands; 4) Rogerian Theory, the primary objective of Rogerian Therapy is to resolve an incongruence to help individuals like George become able to accept and be themselves. To this end a Psychological climate was established in which George could feel free, unconditionally accepted, understood and valued as a person. In this climate George could begin to feel free for perhaps the first time to explore his real feelings and thoughts and to accept hates, angers and "ugly feelings" as parts of himself. As George's self-concept became more congruent with his actual experiences, he could become more self-accepting and more open to new experiences and new perspectives. He could become a better integrated person; 5) In George's case considering the long history of alcoholism in his family of origin, a great deal of family therapy was indicated. Specifically the theory of Adaptive Consequences, in evaluation of an alcoholic family, the therapist must not only look for the maladaptive consequences of the drinking behavior, but also must define the adaptive consequences of drinking. Alcohol abuse often has adaptive consequences that are reinforcing enough to maintain the drinking behavior, regardless of the caustic factors. These adaptive consequences may operate on different levels including interpsychic, intracouple, or to maintain family homeostasis. In George's case it almost seemed that it was predestined that he follow in his parents' footsteps. First to become an alcoholic, and secondly to get into recovery to become part of, and accepted by his family. Many theories can be postulated and pondered in the field of addiction, but the one fact that should never be overlooked when working with an alcoholic or an addict is that there is no better treatment planning than true individualized treatment planning that matches the client's specific needs.

REFERENCES CITED

Ablon, J. 1980. The Significance of Cultural Patterning for the "Alcoholic Family". Family Process, 19(2), 127-144.

Alcoholics Anonymous. Alcoholics Anonymous. New York: Work Publishing, 1939.

Alterman, A., Erdlen, F., and Murphy E. 1981 Alcohol Abuse in the Psychiatric Hospital Population. Addictive Behaviors, 6, 69-73.

Alterman, A. 1985. Substance Abuse in Psychiatric Patients: Etiological, Developmental, and Treatment Considerations. In A. Alterman (Ed.) Psychotherapy and Substance Abuse (pp. 121-136). New York: Plenum

American Psychiatric Association 1980. Diagnostic and Statistical Manual: Mental Disorders (DSM III-R). Washington, D.C.: APA.

American Psychiatric Association 1980. Diagnostic and Statistical Manual of Mental Disorders (3rd Ed.) Washington D.C.: Author.

American Psychiatric Association 1987. Diagnostic and Statistical Manual of Mental Disorders. (Rev. 3rd Ed.) Washington D.C.: Author.

Beck, A.T. 1979. Cognitive Therapy and Emotional Disorders. New York: New American Library.

Beck, A.T. 1973. The Diagnosis and Management of Depression. Philadelphia: University of Pennsylvania Press.

Beck, A.T., Rush, J., Shaw, B.F., and Emery, G. 1979. Cognitive Therapy of Depression New York: Guilford Press.

Beigel, A. and Ghertner, S. 1977. Toward a Social Model: An Assessment of Social Factors with Influence Problem Drinking and it's Treatment. In B. Kissin and H. Begleiter (Eds.) The Biology of Alcoholism: Treatment and Rehabilitation of the Chronic Alcoholic. (Vol. 5, pp. 197-233). New York: Plenum.

Beitman, B.D., Goldfried, M.R., and Norcross, J.C. 1989. The Movement Toward the Psychotherapies: An Overview. American Journal of Psychiatry, 146, 138-147.

Berenson, D. 1976. Alcohol and the Family System. In P. Guerin (Ed.). Family Therapy: Theory and Practice. New York: Gardner Press.

Blume, S.B. 1985. Group Psychotherapy in the Treatment of Alcoholism. In S. Zimberg, J. Wallace, and S.B. Blume (Eds.), Practical Approaches to Alcoholism Psychotherapy (2nd Ed.) (pp. 73-107) New York: Plenum.

Brotman, A.W. Falk, W.E., and Glenberg, A.J. 1987. Pharmacological Treatment of Acute Depressive Subtypes. In H.Y. Meltzer (Ed.) Psychoparmacology: The Third Generation of Progress. (pp. 1031-1040). New York:Raven Press.

Brower, K, MD, Blow, F. Bersford, T. 1989 Treatment Implications of Chemical Dependency Models: An Integrative Approach. Vol. 6, pp 147-157, Journal of Substance Abuse Treatment.

Carson, R., Butcher, J.W. 1992. Abnormal Psychology and Modern Life. 9th Ed. Harper Collins Publishers.

Carter, E. 1977. Generation After Generation: The Long Term Treatment of an Irish Family With Widespread Alcoholism Over Multiple Generations. In P. Papp (Ed.), Family Therapy: Full Length Case Studies. New York: Gardner Press.

Donovan, J.M. 1986. An Etiological Model of Alcoholism. American Journal of Psychiatry 143, 1-11.

Glaser, F.B. 1980. Anybody Got A Match? Treatment Research and the Matching Hypothesis. In G. Edwards and M. Grant (Eds.) Alcoholism Treatment in Transition (pp. 178-196). London: Croom Helm.

Khantzian, E.J. 1984. A Contemporary Psychodynamic Approach to Drug Abuse Treatment. American Journal of Drug and Alcohol Abuse, 12, 213-222.

Kissin, B. 1977. Theory and Practice in the Treatment of Alcoholism. In B. Kissin and H. Begleiter (Eds.) The Biology of Alcoholism: Treatment and Rehabilitation of the Chronic Alcoholic. (Vol. 5, pp. 1-51). New York: Phenum.

Kohut, H. 1971. The Analysis of Self. New York: International Universities Press.

Lawson, G.W., and Lawson, A.W. 1989. Alcoholism and Substance Abuse In Special Populations. Substance Abuse and Psychopathology: The Special Population of the Dual Diagnosis Patient. (pp. 37-43.) Aspen Publications.

Lawson, G.W. 1984. Essentials of Chemical Dependency Counseling. Maryland: Aspen Publications.

Lawson, G.W., Peterson, J.S., and Lawson, A. 1983. Alcoholism and the Family. Maryland: Aspen Systems Corporation.

Lawson, G.W., Cooperrider, C. 1988. Clinical Psychopharmacology. A Practical Reference for Nonmedical Psychotherapists. Maryland: Aspen Publications.

Ludwig, A.M. 1988. Understanding the Alcoholic Mind. New York: Oxford University Press.

Marlatt, G.A. 1985c. Cognitive Assessment and Intervention Procedures for Relapse Prevention. In G.A. Marlatt and J.R. Gordon (Eds.), Relapse Prevention. (pp. 201-279). New York: Guilford Press.

Marlatt, G.A. 1988. Matching Clients to Treatment: Treatment Models and Stages of Change. In D.M. Donovan and G.A. Marlatt (Eds.) Assessment of Addictive Behaviors (pp. 474-483). New York: Guilford Press.

McLellan, A.T. Luborsky, L., Woody, G.E. O'Brien, C.P. and Druley, K.A. 1983. Predicting Response to Alcohol and Drug Abuse Treatments: Role of Psychiatric Severity. Archives of General Psychiatry, 40, 620-625.

Miller, W.R. 1983. Controlled Drinking: A History and a Critical Review. Journal of Studies on Alcohol. 44, 68-83.

Murphy, G.E. 1988. Suicide and Substance Abuse. Archives of General Psychiatry, 45, 593-594.

Page, R.D., and Badgett, S. 1984. Alcoholism Treatment with Environmental Support Contracting. American Journal of Drug and Alcohol Abuse, 10, 589-605.

Polich, J.M., Armor, D.J., and Braiker, H.B. 1981. The Course of Alcoholism: Four Years After Treatment. New York: Wiley.

Rounsaville, B.J., Dolinsky, Z.S., Babor, T.F., and Meyer, R.E. 1987. Psychopathology As A Predictor of Treatment Outcome in Alcoholics. Archives of General Psychiatry, 44, 505-513.

Schuckit, M.A. 1985. Genetics and Risk for Alcoholism. Journal of the American Medical Association, 254, 2614-2617.

Schuckit, M.A. 1986. Genetic and Clinical Implications of Alcoholism and Affective Disorder. American Journal of Psychiatry, 143, 140-147.

Seessel, T.V. 1988. Beyond the Supreme Court Ruling on Alcoholism as Willful Misconduct: It is Up to Congress to Act. Journal of the American Medical Association, 259, 248.

Shaffer, H.J. 1986a. Assessment of Addictive Disorders: The Use of Clinical Reflection and Hypothesis Testing. Psychiatric Clinics of North America, 9, 385-398.

Shaffer, H.J. 1986b. Conceptual Crises and the Addictions: A Philosophy of Science Perspective. Journal of Substance Abuse Treatment, 3, 285-296.

U.S. Department of Mental Health and Human Services, 1994. Assessment and Treatment of Patients with Co-existing Mental Illness and Other Drug Abuse. Rockville, MD.

Vaillant, G.E. 1983. The Natural History of Alcoholism: Causes, Patterns, and Paths to Recovery. Cambridge, MA: Harvard University Press.

Vaillant, G.E. and Milofsky, E.S. 1982. Natural History of Male Alcoholism, Part IV: Paths to Recovery. Archives of General Psychiatry, 39, 127-133.

Vaillant, G.E. 1983. The Natural History of Alcoholism. New York: Wiley.

Wallace, J. 1978. Working With the Preferred Defense Structure of the Recovering Alcoholic. In S. Zimberg, J. Wallace, and S.B. Blume

(Eds.) <u>Practical Approaches to Alcoholism Psychotherapy.</u> (pp. 19-29). New York: Plenum Press.

Woody, G.E., McIlan, T. Luborsky, L., and O'Brien, C.P. 1985. Sociopathy and Sychotherapy Outcome. <u>Archives of General Psychiatry,</u> 42, 1081-1086.